Know Your
BIBLE
Illustrated

Paul Kent | *Full-Color Expanded Edition*
of the Million-Copy Bestseller

BARBOUR
PUBLISHING

Cover design: Faceout Studio, www.faceoutstudio.com
Interior design: Thinkpen Design

Published by Barbour Publishing, Inc., P.O. Box 719, Uhrichsville, Ohio 44683
www.barbourbooks.com

Our mission is to publish and distribute inspirational products offering exceptional value and biblical encouragement to the masses.

Member of the
Evangelical Christian
Publishers Association

Printed in the United States of America.

CONTENTS

INTRODUCTION

Through sixty-six separate books, 1,189 chapters, and hundreds of thousands of words, the Bible shares one extraordinary message: God loves you.

From the first chapter of Genesis, where God creates human beings, through the last chapter of Revelation, where God welcomes anyone to "take the water of life freely" (22:17), the Bible proves God is intimately involved in, familiar with, and concerned about the lives of people. His amazing love is shown in the death of His Son, Jesus Christ, on the cross. That sacrifice for sin allows anyone to be right with God through simple faith in Jesus' work.

These truths are found in the pages of scripture. But sometimes they can be obscured by the vast amount of information the Bible contains. That's why we created *Know Your Bible Illustrated*.

In this book—a fully illustrated version of a small volume that's sold more than a million copies—you'll find brief surveys of all sixty-six Bible books. Each summarizes what that book is about, always within the context of God's love and concern for people.

Every entry follows this outline:

IN TEN WORDS OR LESS: a "nutshell" glance at the book's key theme, immediately following the book's title.

AUTHOR / DATE: who wrote the book, according to the Bible itself or ancient tradition, and when the book was written or the time the book covers.

DETAILS, PLEASE: a synopsis of the key people, events, and messages covered in the book.

QUOTABLE: one, two, or several key verses from the book.

UNIQUE AND UNUSUAL: facts—some serious, some less so—that make the book stand out.

SO WHAT? an inspirational or devotional thought for each book.

Your Bible is certainly worth knowing. Use this book to begin a journey of discovery that could truly change your life!

GENESIS

God creates the world and chooses a special people.

AUTHOR / DATE

Not stated but traditionally attributed to Moses. Moses lived around the 1400s BC, but the events of Genesis date to the very beginning of time.

DETAILS, PLEASE

The Bible's first book never explains God; it simply assumes His existence: "In the beginning God. . ." (1:1). Chapters 1 and 2 describe how God created the universe and everything in it simply by speaking: "God said. . .and it was so" (1:6–7, 9, 11, 14–15). Humans, however, received special handling, as "God formed man of the dust of the ground, and breathed into his nostrils the breath of life" (2:7), and woman was crafted from a rib of man. Those first two people, Adam and Eve, lived in perfection but ruined paradise by disobeying God at the urging of a "subtil" (crafty, 3:1) serpent. Sin throws humans into a moral free-fall as the world's first child—Cain—murders his brother Abel. People become so bad that God decides to flood the entire planet, saving only the righteous Noah, his family, and an ark (boat) full of animals. After the earth repopulates, God chooses a man named Abram as patriarch of a specially blessed people, later called "Israel" after an alternative name of Abram's grandson Jacob. Genesis ends with Jacob's son Joseph, by a miraculous chain of events, ruling in Egypt—setting up the events of the following book of Exodus.

Jacob wrestles with a mysterious man—and later says, "I have seen God face to face." The angelic being renames Jacob *Israel,* meaning "he struggles with God" (Genesis 32:22–32).

QUOTABLE

- *God said, Let there be light: and there was light. (1:3)*
- *The Lord said unto Cain, Where is Abel thy brother? And he said, I know not: Am I my brother's keeper? (4:9)*
- *Noah found grace in the eyes of the Lord. (6:8)*
- *He [Abram] believed in the Lord; and he counted it to him for righteousness. (15:6)*
- *Is any thing too hard for the Lord? (18:14)*
- *Ye thought evil against me; but God meant it unto good, to bring to pass, as it is this day, to save much people alive. (50:20)*

UNIQUE AND UNUSUAL

Genesis quickly introduces the concept of one God in multiple persons, a concept later called the Trinity: "God said, Let *us* make man in *our* image, after *our* likeness" (1:26, emphasis added). Also early on, God gives a hint of Jesus' future suffering and victory when He curses the serpent for deceiving Eve: "I will put enmity between thee and the woman, and between thy seed and her seed; it shall bruise thy head, and thou shalt bruise his heel" (3:15).

SO WHAT?

Genesis answers the great question "Where did I come from?" Knowing the answer can give us meaning in a world that's otherwise hard to figure out.

We don't know exactly what kind of fruit it was. . . but Adam and Eve's disobedience led to major trouble for the human race (Genesis 3).

EXODUS

God delivers His people, the Israelites, from slavery in Egypt.

AUTHOR / DATE

Not stated but traditionally attributed to Moses. In Exodus 34:27 God tells Moses, "Write thou these words," and Jesus, in Mark 12:26, quotes from Exodus as "the book of Moses." Written in approximately the mid-1400s BC.

DETAILS, PLEASE

The Israelites prosper in Egypt, having settled there at the invitation of Abraham's great-grandson Joseph, who entered the country as a slave and rose to second in command. When Joseph dies, a new pharaoh sees the burgeoning family as a threat—and makes the people his slaves. God hears the Israelites' groaning, remembering "his covenant with Abraham, with Isaac, and with Jacob" (2:24) and raising up Moses as their deliverer. God speaks through a burning bush, and Moses reluctantly agrees to demand the Israelites' release from Pharaoh. To break Pharaoh's will, God sends ten plagues on Egypt, ending with the death of every firstborn child—except those of the Israelites. They put sacrificial blood on their doorposts, causing the Lord to "pass over" (12:13) their homes. Pharaoh finally allows the Israelites to leave the country (the "Exodus"), and God parts the Red Sea for the people, who are being pursued by Egyptian soldiers. At Mount Sinai, God delivers the Ten Commandments, rules for worship, and laws to change the family into a nation. When Moses delays on the mountain, the people begin worshipping a golden calf, bringing a plague upon themselves. Moses returns to restore order, and Exodus ends with the people continuing their journey to the "promised land" of Canaan, following God's "pillar of cloud" by day and "pillar of fire" by night.

QUOTABLE

- *God said unto Moses, I AM THAT I AM: and he said, Thus shalt thou say unto the children of Israel, I AM hath sent me unto you. (3:14)*
- *Thus saith the LORD, Let my people go. (8:1)*
- *When I see the blood, I will pass over you. (12:13)*
- *Thou shalt have no other gods before me. (20:3)*

Flames from an explosion light up the evening sky —a modern hint of God's miraculous sign for the ancient Israelites leaving Egypt (Exodus 13:21–22).

- *Thou shalt not kill. (20:13)*
- *Thou shalt not commit adultery. (20:14)*
- *The LORD said unto Moses, Whosoever hath sinned against me, him will I blot out of my book. (32:33)*

UNIQUE AND UNUSUAL

God told the Israelites to celebrate the "Passover" with a special meal of bread made without yeast (12:14–15). Three thousand years later, Jewish people still commemorate the event.

A five-year-old Jewish boy holds the unleavened "matzah" bread of the Passover celebration.

SO WHAT?

The story of redemption is on clear display in Exodus as God rescues His people from their slavery in Egypt. In the same way, Jesus breaks our bonds of sin (Hebrews 2:14–15).

LEVITICUS

A holy God explains how to worship Him.

AUTHOR / DATE

Not stated but traditionally attributed to Moses. Written in approximately the mid-1400s BC.

DETAILS, PLEASE

Leviticus, meaning "about the Levites," describes how that family line should lead the Israelites in worship. The book provides ceremonial laws as opposed to the moral laws of Exodus, describing offerings to God, dietary restrictions, and purification rites. Special holy days—including the Sabbath, Passover, and Day of Atonement (Yom Kippur)—are commanded. The family of Aaron, Moses' brother, is

God's law said any sacrifice of bulls, goats, or sheep should be of a "male without blemish" (Leviticus 1:10). Jesus met that demand, too.

ordained as Israel's formal priesthood. Leviticus lists several blessings for obedience and many more punishments for disobedience.

QUOTABLE

- *Ye shall be holy; for I [God] am holy. (11:44)*
- *The goat, on which the lot fell to be the scapegoat, shall be presented alive before the LORD, to make an atonement with him. (16:10)*
- *The life of the flesh is in the blood. . .it is the blood that maketh an atonement for the soul. (17:11)*
- *I will walk among you, and will be your God, and ye shall be my people. (26:12)*

UNIQUE AND UNUSUAL

Leviticus's blood sacrifices are contrasted with Jesus' death on the cross by the writer of Hebrews: "[Jesus] needeth not daily, as those high priests, to offer up sacrifice. . .for this he did once, when he offered up himself" (7:27).

SO WHAT?

Though we don't live under the rules of Leviticus, we still serve a holy God—and should treat Him as such.

NUMBERS
Faithless Israelites wander forty years in the wilderness of Sinai.

AUTHOR / DATE

Not stated but traditionally attributed to Moses. Written in approximately 1400 BC.

DETAILS, PLEASE

Numbers begins with a census—hence the book's name. Fourteen months after the Israelites escape Egypt, they number 603,550 men, not including the Levites. This mass of people, the newly formed nation of Israel, begins a march of approximately two hundred miles to the "promised land" of Canaan—a journey that will take decades to complete. The delay is God's punishment of the people, who complain about food and water, rebel against Moses, and hesitate to enter Canaan because of powerful people already living there. God decrees that this entire generation will die in the wilderness, leaving the Promised Land to a new generation of more obedient Israelites.

QUOTABLE

- *When the dew fell upon the camp in the night, the manna fell upon it. (11:9)*
- *If the LORD delight in us, then he will bring us into this land, and give it us; a land which floweth with milk and honey. (14:8)*
- *The LORD is longsuffering, and of great mercy, forgiving iniquity and transgression. (14:18)*
- *I am the LORD your God, which brought you out of the land of Egypt, to be your God: I am the LORD your God. (15:41)*

UNIQUE AND UNUSUAL

Even Moses misses out on the Promised Land, punishment for disobeying God by striking, rather than speaking to, a rock from which
water would miraculously appear (20:1–13).

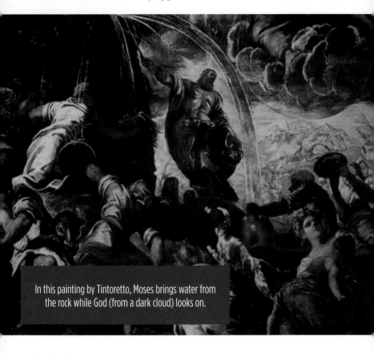

In this painting by Tintoretto, Moses brings water from
the rock while God (from a dark cloud) looks on.

SO WHAT?

God hates sin and punishes it. We can be thankful that Jesus took that
punishment for us.

DEUTERONOMY

Moses reminds the Israelites of their history and God's laws.

AUTHOR / DATE

Traditionally attributed to Moses, an idea supported by Deuteronomy 31:9: "Moses wrote this law, and delivered it unto the priests. . .and unto all the elders of Israel." Chapter 34, recording Moses' death, was probably written by his successor, Joshua. Written approximately 1400 BC.

DETAILS, PLEASE

With a name meaning "second law," Deuteronomy records Moses' final words as the Israelites prepare to enter the Promised Land. Forty years have passed since God handed down His laws on Mount Sinai, and the entire generation that experienced that momentous event has died. So Moses reminds the new generation both of God's commands and of their national history as they ready their entry into Canaan. The invasion will occur under Joshua, as Moses will only *see* the Promised Land from Mount Nebo. "So Moses the servant of the LORD died there. . . . And he [God] buried him in a valley in the land of Moab. . .but no man knoweth of his sepulchre unto this day" (34:5–6). Moses was 120 years old.

This church atop Mount Nebo protects the much older Basilica of Moses.

17

QUOTABLE

- *Hear, O Israel: The L*ORD *our God is one L*ORD*. (6:4)*
- *Thou shalt love the L*ORD *thy God with all thine heart, and with all thy soul, and with all thy might. (6:5)*
- *The L*ORD *thy God is a jealous God among you. (6:15)*
- *Thou art an holy people unto the L*ORD *thy God: the L*ORD *thy God hath chosen thee to be a special people unto himself, above all people that are upon the face of the earth. (7:6)*
- *The L*ORD *shall cause thine enemies that rise up against thee to be smitten before thy face: they shall come out against thee one way, and flee before thee seven ways. (28:7)*
- *And there arose not a prophet since in Israel like unto Moses, whom the L*ORD *knew face to face. (34:10)*

UNIQUE AND UNUSUAL

The New Testament quotes from Deuteronomy dozens of times, including three times in the story of Jesus' temptation in the wilderness in Matthew 4:1–11. The Lord defeated Satan by restating Deuteronomy 8:3 ("Man shall not live by bread alone, but by every word that proceedeth out of the mouth of God"); 6:16 ("Thou shalt not tempt the Lord thy God"); and 6:13 ("Thou shalt worship the Lord thy God, and him only shalt thou serve").

The Ten Commandments, most commonly found in Exodus 20, are restated in full in Deuteronomy 5.

SO WHAT?

Deuteronomy makes clear that God's rules and expectations aren't meant to limit and frustrate us but instead to benefit us: "Hear therefore, O Israel, and observe to do it; that it may be well with thee, and that ye may increase mightily, as the L*ORD* God of thy fathers hath promised thee, in the land that floweth with milk and honey" (6:3).

Most depictions of Christ's temptation in the desert depict dramatic confrontations with an embodied Satan, but as shown in this painting by Kramskoi, the struggle may also have been internal and lonely.

JOSHUA

The Israelites capture and settle
the promised land of Canaan.

AUTHOR / DATE

Traditionally attributed to Joshua
himself, except for the final five
verses (24:29–33), which describe
Joshua's death and legacy. Written
approximately 1375 BC.

DETAILS, PLEASE

With Moses and an entire generation of disobedient Israelites dead,
God tells Joshua to lead the people
into Canaan, their promised land.
In Jericho, the first major obstacle,
the prostitute Rahab helps Israelite
spies and earns protection from the
destruction of the city: God knocks
its walls flat as Joshua's army
marches outside, blowing trumpets
and shouting. Joshua leads a success-
ful military campaign to clear idol-
worshipping people—Hittites,
Amorites, Canaanites, Perizzites,
Hivites, and Jebusites—from the
land. At one point, God answers
Joshua's prayer to make the sun
stand still, allowing more time to

A statue of Baal, one of the pagan
gods whose worship caused so many
problems for the Israelites.

complete a battle (10:1–15). Major cities subdued, Joshua divides the land among the twelve tribes of Israel, reminding the people to stay true to the God who led them home: "Now therefore put away. . .the strange gods which are among you, and incline your heart unto the LORD God of Israel" (24:23).

QUOTABLE

- *Be strong and of a good courage; be not afraid, neither be thou dismayed: for the LORD thy God is with thee whithersoever thou goest. (1:9)*
- *Loose thy shoe from off thy foot; for the place whereon thou standest is holy. (5:15)*
- *Joshua went unto him, and said unto him, Art thou for us, or for our adversaries? And he said, Nay; but as captain of the host of the LORD am I now come. (5:13–14)*
- *So the LORD was with Joshua; and his fame was noised throughout all the country. (6:27)*
- *And there was no day like that before it or after it, that the LORD hearkened unto the voice of a man: for the LORD fought for Israel. (10:14)*
- *And the LORD gave unto Israel all the land which he sware to give unto their fathers; and they possessed it, and dwelt therein. (21:43)*
- *One man of you shall chase a thousand: for the LORD your God, he it is that fighteth for you, as he hath promised you. (23:10)*
- *Choose you this day whom ye will serve. . .as for me and my house, we will serve the LORD. (24:15)*
- *The people said unto Joshua, The LORD our God will we serve, and his voice will we obey. (24:24)*

UNIQUE AND UNUSUAL

Joshua is one of few major Bible characters who seemed to do everything right—he was a strong leader, completely committed to God, who never fell into recorded sin or disobedience. Only one mistake mars his record: Joshua's experience with the Gibeonites, one of the local groups he should have destroyed. Fearing for their lives, they appeared before Joshua dressed in old clothes, carrying dry, moldy bread, claiming they had come from a faraway land. Joshua and the Israelite leaders "asked not counsel at the mouth of the LORD" (9:14) and agreed to a peace treaty. When Joshua learned the truth, he honored his agreement with the Gibeonites—but made them slaves.

Joshua's only recorded failure involved neighbors who claimed to have traveled from far away.

SO WHAT?

Joshua shows over and over how God blesses His people. The Promised Land was His gift to them, as were the military victories that He engineered.

JUDGES

Israel goes through cycles of sin, suffering, and salvation.

AUTHOR / DATE

Unknown; some suggest the prophet Samuel. Written approximately 1050 BC, covering events that occurred as far back as 1375 BC.

DETAILS, PLEASE

After Joshua's death, the Israelites lose momentum in driving pagan people out of the Promised Land. "The children of Benjamin did not drive out the Jebusites that inhabited Jerusalem" (1:21) is a statement characteristic of many tribes, which allow idol worshippers to stay in their midst—with tragic results. "Ye have not obeyed my voice," God says to His people. "They shall be as thorns in your sides, and their gods shall be a snare unto you" (2:2–3). That's exactly what happens, as the Israelites begin a cycle of worshipping idols, suffering punishment by attackers, crying to God for help, and receiving God's aid in the form of a human judge (or "deliverer") who restores order. Lesser-known judges include Othniel, Ehud, Tola, Jair, and Jephthah, while more familiar figures are Deborah, the only female judge, who led a military victory against the Canaanites; Gideon, who tested God's will with a fleece and defeated the armies of Midian; and the amazingly strong Samson, who defeated the Philistines. Samson's great weakness—his love for unsavory women such as Delilah—led to his downfall and death in a Philistine temple.

The modern Israeli army—following in the footsteps of its ancient counterpart—patrols the village of Awarta.

QUOTABLE

- *They forsook the LORD God of their fathers, which brought them out of the land of Egypt, and followed other gods, of the gods of the people that were round about them. (2:12)*
- *The LORD raised up judges, which delivered them out of the hand of those that spoiled them. (2:16)*
- *The LORD said unto Gideon, The people that are with thee are too many for me to give the Midianites into their hands, lest Israel vaunt themselves against me, saying, Mine own hand hath saved me. (7:2)*

UNIQUE AND UNUSUAL

Several judges had unusual families by today's standards: Jair had thirty sons (10:4), Abdon had forty sons (12:14), and Ibzan had thirty sons and thirty daughters (12:9). Jephthah had only one child, a daughter, whom he foolishly vowed to sacrifice to God in exchange for a military victory (11:30–40).

There are "only" seventeen people in this entire family portrait of three generations. Some of the judges had three times that many children!

SO WHAT?

The ancient Israelites got into trouble when they "did that which was right in [their] own eyes" (17:6; 21:25) rather than what God wanted them to do. Don't make the same mistake yourself!

RUTH
Loyal daughter-in-law pictures
God's faithfulness, love, and care.

AUTHOR / DATE

Not stated; some suggest Samuel. Ruth, the great-grandmother of King David (who reigned approximately 1010–970 BC), probably lived around 1100 BC.

DETAILS, PLEASE

Ruth, a Gentile woman, marries into a Jewish family. When all of the men of the family die, Ruth shows loyalty to her mother-in-law, Naomi, staying with her and scavenging food to keep them alive. As Ruth gleans barley in a field of the wealthy Boaz, he takes an interest in her and orders his workers to watch over her. Naomi recognizes Boaz as her late husband's relative and encourages Ruth to pursue him as a "kinsman redeemer," one who weds a relative's widow to continue a family line. Boaz marries Ruth, starting a prominent family.

QUOTABLE

- *Whither thou goest, I will go; and where thou lodgest, I will lodge: thy people shall be my people, and thy God my God. (1:16)*

UNIQUE AND UNUSUAL

Ruth, from the pagan land of Moab, married a Jewish man and became the great-grandmother of Israel's greatest king, David—and an ancestor of Jesus Christ.

Ruth makes the decision to remain a faithful "daughter" to her mother-in-law, Naomi.

SO WHAT?

We can trust God to provide what we need, when we need it—and to work out our lives in ways that are better than we ever imagined.

1 SAMUEL

Israel's twelve tribes unite under a king.

AUTHOR / DATE

Not stated. Samuel himself was likely involved, though some of the history of 1 Samuel occurs after the prophet's death. Approximately 1100–1000 BC.

DETAILS, PLEASE

An infertile woman, Hannah, begs God for a son, promising to return him to the Lord's service. Samuel is born and soon sent to the temple to serve under the aging priest, Eli. Upon Eli's death, Samuel serves as judge, or deliverer, of Israel, subduing the nation's fearsome enemy, the Philistines. As Samuel ages, Israel's tribal leaders reject his sinful sons and ask for a king. Samuel warns that a king will tax the people and force them into service, but they insist and God tells Samuel to anoint the notably tall and handsome Saul as Israel's first ruler. King Saul starts well but begins making poor choices—and when he offers a sacrifice to God, a job reserved for priests, Samuel tells Saul that he will be replaced. Saul's successor will be a shepherd named David, who with God's help kills a giant Philistine warrior named Goliath and becomes Israel's hero. The jealous king seeks to kill David, who runs for his life. David rejects opportunities to kill Saul himself, saying, "I would not stretch forth mine hand against the LORD's anointed" (26:23). At the end of 1 Samuel, Saul dies battling the Philistines, making way for David to become king.

The young Samuel answers the voice of God in the night.

QUOTABLE

- *The LORD said unto Samuel. . .they have not rejected thee, but they have rejected me, that I should not reign over them. (8:7)*
- *Behold, to obey is better than sacrifice, and to hearken than the fat of rams. (15:22)*
- *Then said David to the Philistine [Goliath], Thou comest to me with a sword, and with a spear, and with a shield: but I come to thee in the name of the LORD of hosts, the God of the armies of Israel, whom thou hast defied. (17:45)*

In going his own way and refusing advice, Saul may have grown as stubborn as the animals he once cared for.

UNIQUE AND UNUSUAL

The future King Saul is a donkey herder (9:5) who tries to hide from his own coronation (10:21–22). As king, Saul breaks his own law by asking a medium to call up the spirit of the dead Samuel (chapter 28).

SO WHAT?

Selfish choices—such as the Israelites' request for a king and Saul's decision to offer a sacrifice he had no business making—can have heavy, even tragic, consequences.

2 SAMUEL

David becomes Israel's greatest king—but with major flaws.

AUTHOR / DATE

Unknown but not Samuel—since the events of the book take place after his death. Some suggest Abiathar the priest (15:35). Written approximately 1010–970 BC, the reign of King David.

DETAILS, PLEASE

When King Saul dies, David is made king by the southern Jewish tribe of Judah. Seven years later, after the death of Saul's son Ish-bosheth, king of the northern tribes, David becomes ruler of all Israel. Capturing Jerusalem from the Jebusites, David creates a new capital for his unified nation, and God promises David, "Your throne will be established forever" (7:16 NIV). Military victories make Israel strong, but when David stays home from battle one spring, he commits adultery with a beautiful neighbor, Bathsheba. Then he has her husband—one of his soldiers—murdered. The prophet Nathan confronts David with a story of a rich man who steals a poor man's sheep. David is furious until Nathan announces, "Thou art the man" (12:7). Chastened, David repents and God forgives his sins—but their consequences will affect David powerfully. The baby conceived in the tryst dies, and David's family begins to splinter apart. One of David's sons, Amnon, rapes his half sister, and a second son, Absalom—full brother to the violated girl—kills Amnon in revenge. Absalom then conspires to steal the kingdom from David, causing his father to flee for his life. When Absalom dies in battle with David's men, David grieves so deeply that he offends his soldiers. Ultimately, David returns to

Jerusalem to reassert his kingship. He also raises another son born to Bathsheba—Solomon.

QUOTABLE

- *How are the mighty fallen in the midst of the battle! (1:25)*
- *Who am I, O Lord GOD? and what is my house, that thou hast brought me hitherto? (7:18)*
- *O my son Absalom, my son, my son Absalom! would God I had died for thee, O Absalom, my son, my son! (18:33)*

UNIQUE AND UNUSUAL

David's nephew killed a Philistine "of great stature, that had on every hand six fingers, and on every foot six toes" (21:20). David's top soldier, Adino, once killed eight hundred men single-handedly (23:8).

SO WHAT?

King David's story highlights the vital importance of the choices we make. Who would have guessed that such a great man could fall into such terrible sin?

Bathsheba, as depicted by Jan Massys. The painting is displayed in the Louvre in Paris.

1 KINGS

Israel divides into rival northern and southern nations.

AUTHOR / DATE

Not stated and unknown; one early tradition claimed Jeremiah wrote 1 and 2 Kings. Covering events from about 970 to 850 BC, 1 Kings was probably written sometime after the Babylonian destruction of Jerusalem in 586 BC.

DETAILS, PLEASE

King David, in declining health, names Solomon, his son with Bathsheba, successor. After David's death, God speaks to Solomon in a dream, offering him anything he'd like—and Solomon chooses wisdom. God gives Solomon great wisdom, along with much power and wealth. The new king soon builds God a permanent temple in Jerusalem, and the Lord visits Solomon again to promise blessings for obedience and trouble for disobedience. Sadly, Solomon's wisdom fails him, as he marries seven hundred women, many of them foreigners who turn his heart to idols. When Solomon dies, his son Rehoboam foolishly antagonizes the people of Israel, and ten northern tribes form their own nation under Jeroboam, a former official of Solomon's. Two southern tribes continue under Solomon's line in a nation called Judah. Jeroboam begins badly, initiating idol worship in the north; many wicked rulers follow. Judah will also have many poor leaders, though occasional kings, such as Asa and Jehoshaphat, follow the Lord. First Kings introduces the prophet Elijah, who confronts the evil King Ahab and Queen Jezebel of Israel regarding their worship of the false god Baal. In God's power, Elijah defeats 450 false prophets in a dramatic contest on Mount Carmel.

Driven into the wilderness after Queen Jezebel threatened his life, Elijah was fed by an angel.

QUOTABLE

- *The days of David drew nigh that he should die; and he charged Solomon his son, saying, I go the way of all the earth: be thou strong therefore, and shew thyself a man. (2:1–2)*
- *Give therefore thy servant an understanding heart to judge thy people, that I may discern between good and bad: for who is able to judge this thy so great a people? (3:9)*
- *Hear me, O LORD, hear me, that this people may know that thou art the LORD God, and that thou hast turned their heart back again. (18:37)*

UNIQUE AND UNUSUAL

Scholars say 1 and 2 Kings were originally a single volume and were split in half to allow for copying onto normal-sized scrolls.

SO WHAT?

Solomon's example provides a strong warning: Even the most blessed person can drift from God and make big mistakes.

This 1895 Bible card depicts "the sin of Solomon." Influenced by his wives, he turned to false forms of worship.

2 KINGS

Both Jewish nations are destroyed
for their disobedience to God.

AUTHOR / DATE

Not stated and unknown; one early tradition claimed Jeremiah wrote
1 and 2 Kings. Covering about three hundred years from the 800s
BC on, 2 Kings was probably written sometime after the Babylonian
destruction of Jerusalem in 586 BC.

DETAILS, PLEASE

The story of 1 Kings continues, with more bad rulers, a handful of
good ones, some familiar prophets, and the ultimate downfall of the
two Jewish nations. Early in 2 Kings, Elijah becomes the second man
(after Enoch in Genesis 5:24) to go straight to heaven without dying.
His successor, Elisha, performs many miracles and shares God's word
with the "average people" of Israel. The northern kingdom's rulers
are entirely wicked, and Israel, under its last king, Hoshea, is "carried. . .away into Assyria" (17:6) in 722 BC. Judah, with occasional
good kings such as Hezekiah and Josiah, lasts a few years longer—but
in 586 BC the southern kingdom's capital of Jerusalem "was broken
up" (25:4) by Babylonian armies under King Nebuchadnezzar.
Besides taking everything valuable from the temple and the Jewish
king's palace, the Babylonians also "carried away all Jerusalem, and all
the princes, and all the mighty men of valour, even ten thousand captives, and all the craftsmen and smiths" (24:14). Ending on a slight up
note, 2 Kings describes a new king of Babylon, Evil-merodach, showing kindness to Jehoiachin, the last real king of Judah, by giving him a
place of honor in the Babylonian court.

QUOTABLE

- *Behold, there appeared a chariot of fire, and horses of fire, and parted them both asunder; and Elijah went up by a whirlwind into heaven. (2:11)*
- *The LORD rejected all the seed of Israel, and afflicted them, and delivered them into the hand of spoilers, until he had cast them out of his sight. (17:20)*
- *So Judah was carried away out of their land. (25:21)*

UNIQUE AND UNUSUAL

Isaiah, who wrote a long prophecy that appears later in the Old Testament, is prominent in 2 Kings 19. One of Judah's best kings, Josiah, was only eight years old when he took the throne (22:1).

SO WHAT?

Both Israel and Judah found that there were terrible consequences to sin. Even bad examples can be helpful if we decide not to do the things that bring us trouble.

An 1850s woodcut of Elijah heading heavenward in a chariot of fire.

1 CHRONICLES

King David's reign is detailed and analyzed.

AUTHOR /DATE

Not stated but traditionally attributed to Ezra the priest. Covers the history of Israel from about 1010 BC (the death of King Saul) to about 970 BC (the death of King David).

DETAILS, PLEASE

First Chronicles provides a history of Israel, going as far back as Adam. By the eleventh chapter, the story turns to Israel's greatest king, David, with special emphasis on his leadership of national worship. Another important focus is on God's promise that David would have an eternal kingly line through his descendant Jesus Christ.

QUOTABLE

• *I will settle him in mine house and in my kingdom for ever: and his throne shall be established for evermore. (17:14)*

UNIQUE AND UNUSUAL

First Chronicles covers much of the same information as 2 Samuel, but without some of the seedier aspects of David's life—such as his adultery with Bathsheba and the engineered killing of her husband, Uriah.

SO WHAT?

The positive spin of 1 Chronicles was designed to remind the Jews that despite their punishment for sin, they were still God's special people. When God makes a promise, He keeps it.

2 CHRONICLES

The history of Israel from Solomon to division to destruction.

AUTHOR / DATE

Not stated but traditionally attributed to Ezra the priest. Covers Israelite history from about 970 BC (the accession of King Solomon) to the 500s BC (when exiled Jews returned to Jerusalem).

DETAILS, PLEASE

David's son Solomon is made king, builds the temple, and becomes one of the most prominent rulers ever. But when he dies, the Jewish nation divides. In the remainder of 2 Chronicles, the various kings of the relatively godlier southern nation of Judah are profiled right down to the destruction of Jerusalem by the Babylonians. The book ends with the Persian king Cyrus allowing Jews to rebuild the devastated temple.

QUOTABLE

- *Lord God of Israel, there is no God like thee in the heaven, nor in the earth; which keepest covenant, and shewest mercy unto thy servants, that walk before thee with all their hearts. (6:14)*

UNIQUE AND UNUSUAL

Continuing the positive spin of 1 Chronicles (the two books were originally one), 2 Chronicles ends with two verses that exactly repeat the first three verses of Ezra.

SO WHAT?

God's punishment isn't intended to hurt people but to bring them back to Him.

EZRA

Spiritual renewal begins after the Jews return from exile.

AUTHOR / DATE

Not stated but traditionally attributed to Ezra the priest (7:11). Written approximately 530 BC to the mid-400s BC.

DETAILS, PLEASE

About a half century after Babylonians sacked Jerusalem and carried Jews into captivity, Persia is the new world power. King Cyrus allows a group of exiles to return to Judah to rebuild the temple. Some 42,000 people return and resettle the land. About seventy years later, Ezra is part of a smaller group that also returns. He teaches the law to the people, who have fallen away from God to the point of intermarrying with nearby pagan nations, something that was strictly forbidden by Moses (Deuteronomy 7:1–3).

QUOTABLE

- *Who is there among you of all his people? his God be with him, and let him go up to Jerusalem, which is in Judah, and build the house of the LORD God of Israel, (he is the God,) which is in Jerusalem. (1:3)*
- *Ezra had prepared his heart to seek the law of the LORD, and to do it, and to teach in Israel statutes and judgments. (7:10)*
- *Blessed be the LORD God of our fathers, which hath put such a thing as this in the king's heart, to beautify the house of the LORD which is in Jerusalem. (7:27)*
- *O my God, I am ashamed and blush to lift up my face to thee, my God: for our iniquities are increased over our head, and our trespass is grown up unto the heavens. (9:6)*

UNIQUE AND UNUSUAL

Though God has said, "I hate divorce" (Malachi 2:16 NIV), Ezra urged Jewish men to separate from their foreign wives.

Marriages, which should have been inviolate, were ended in Ezra's time because God was not part of them from the start.

SO WHAT?

In Ezra, God shows His willingness to offer a second chance—allowing a nation that had been punished for disobedience to have a fresh start. Guess what? He's still in the second-chance business.

NEHEMIAH

Returning Jewish exiles rebuild the broken walls of Jerusalem.

AUTHOR / DATE

"The words of Nehemiah" (1:1), though Jewish tradition says those words were put on paper by Ezra. Written approximately 445 BC.

DETAILS, PLEASE

Nehemiah serves as "the king's cupbearer" (1:11) in Shushan, Persia. As a Jew, he's disturbed to learn that even though exiles have been back in Judah for nearly a hundred years, they have not rebuilt the city's walls, devastated by the Babylonians in 586 BC. Nehemiah asks and receives the king's permission to return to Jerusalem, where he leads a team of builders—against much pagan opposition—in reconstructing the walls in only fifty-two days. The quick work on the project shocks the Jews' enemies, who "perceived that this work was wrought of our God" (6:16).

QUOTABLE

- *I beseech thee, O LORD God of heaven, the great and terrible God, that keepeth covenant and mercy for them that love him and observe his commandments. (1:5)*
- *They said, Let us rise up and build. So they strengthened their hands for this good work. (2:18)*
- *Think upon me, my God, for good, according to all that I have done for this people. (5:19)*

UNIQUE AND UNUSUAL

Indignant over some fellow Jews' intermarriage with pagans, Nehemiah "cursed them, and smote certain of them, and plucked off their hair" (13:25).

SO WHAT?

Nehemiah's success in rebuilding Jerusalem's walls provides many leadership principles for today—especially his consistent focus on prayer.

An illustration of Nehemiah rebuilding the walls from *Sunrays,* a quarterly magazine, published in 1908.

ESTHER

Beautiful Jewish girl becomes queen,
saves fellow Jews from slaughter.

AUTHOR / DATE

Not stated but perhaps Ezra or Nehemiah. Approximately 486–465 BC,
during the reign of King Ahasuerus of Persia. Esther became queen
around 479 BC.

DETAILS, PLEASE

In a nationwide beauty contest, young Esther becomes queen of Persia
without revealing her Jewish heritage. When a royal official plots to kill
every Jew in the country, Esther risks her own life to request the king's
protection. The king, pleased with Esther, is shocked by his official's
plan and has the man hanged—while decreeing that the Jews should
defend themselves against the planned slaughter. Esther's people pre-
vail and commemorate the event with a holiday called Purim.

QUOTABLE

- *Esther obtained favour in the sight of all them that looked upon her. (2:15)*
- *Who knoweth whether thou art come to the kingdom for such a time as
  this? (4:14)*
- *What is thy request? even to the half of the kingdom it shall be performed.
  (5:6)*
- *The decree of Esther confirmed these matters of Purim; and it was written
  in the book. (9:32)*

UNIQUE AND UNUSUAL

God's name is never mentioned in the book of Esther. Neither is prayer, though Esther asks her fellow Jews to fast for her before she approaches the king (4:16).

SO WHAT?

When we find ourselves in bad situations, it may be for the same reason Esther did—to accomplish something good.

Esther in the palace of the Persian king, from a nineteenth-century painting by Léon Benouville.

JOB

God allows human suffering for His own purposes.

AUTHOR / DATE

Not stated. Date is unclear, but many believe Job is one of the oldest stories in the Bible, perhaps from approximately 2000 BC.

DETAILS, PLEASE

Head of a large family, Job is a wealthy farmer from a place called Uz. He's "perfect and upright" (1:1)—so much so, that God calls Satan's attention to him. The devil, unimpressed, asks and receives God's permission to attack Job's possessions—and wipes out thousands of sheep, camels, oxen, donkeys, and, worst of all, Job's ten children. Despite Satan's attack, Job keeps his faith. Satan then receives God's permission to attack Job's health—but in spite of terrible physical suffering, Job refuses to "curse God, and die" as his wife suggests (2:9). Before long, though, Job begins to question why God would allow him—a good man—to suffer so severely. Job's suffering is worsened by the arrival of

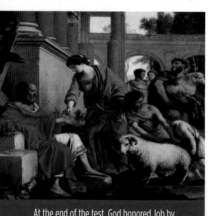

At the end of the test, God honored Job by restoring his wealth twofold—and giving him ten more children.

In the depth of his suffering Job still refused to "curse God, and die." Instead he only wanted to understand why such calamity had come upon him.

four "friends" who begin to accuse him of causing his own trouble by secret sin. "Is not thy wickedness great?" asks Eliphaz the Temanite (22:5). In the end, God Himself speaks, vindicating Job before his friends and also addressing the overarching issue of human suffering. God doesn't explain Job's suffering but asks a series of questions that shows His vast knowledge—implying that Job should simply trust God's way. And Job does, telling God, "I know that thou canst do every thing" (42:2). By story's end, God has restored Job's health, possessions, and family, giving him ten more children.

QUOTABLE

- *Naked came I out of my mother's womb, and naked shall I return thither: the LORD gave, and the LORD hath taken away; blessed be the name of the LORD. (1:21)*
- *My days are swifter than a weaver's shuttle, and are spent without hope. (7:6)*
- *Wherefore then hast thou brought me forth out of the womb? Oh that I had given up the ghost, and no eye had seen me! (10:18)*
- *Man that is born of a woman is of few days, and full of trouble. (14:1)*
- *Miserable comforters are ye all. (16:2)*
- *Behold, my witness is in heaven, and my record is on high. (16:19)*
- *He knoweth the way that I take: when he hath tried me, I shall come forth as gold. (23:10)*
- *I abhor myself, and repent in dust and ashes. (42:6)*

UNIQUE AND UNUSUAL

The book of Job pictures Satan coming into God's presence (1:6). It also gives a clear Old Testament hint of Jesus' work when Job says, "I know that my redeemer liveth, and that he shall stand at the latter day upon the earth" (19:25).

SO WHAT?

Trouble isn't necessarily a sign of sin in a person's life. It may be something God allows to draw us closer to Him.

PSALMS

Ancient Jewish songbook showcases prayers, praise—
and complaints—to God.

AUTHORS / DATE

Various, with nearly half attributed to King David. Other names noted
include Solomon, Moses, Asaph, Ethan, and the sons of Korah. Many
psalms don't mention an author. Written approximately the 1400s
BC (Moses' time) through the 500s BC (the time of the Jews' Babylonian exile).

DETAILS, PLEASE

Over several centuries, God led various individuals to compose emo-
tionally charged poems—of which 150 were later compiled into the
book we know as Psalms. Many of the psalms are described as "of
David," meaning they could be *by*, *for*, or *about* Israel's great king.
Highlights of the book include the "Shepherd Psalm" (23), which
describes God as protector and provider; David's cry for forgiveness
after his sin with Bathsheba (51); psalms of praise (100 is a powerful
example); and the celebration of scripture found in Psalm 119, with
almost all of the 176 verses making some reference to God's laws,
statutes, commandments, precepts, word, and the like. Some psalms,
called "imprecatory," call for God's judgment on enemies (see Psalms
69 and 109, for example). Many psalms express agony of spirit on the
writer's part—but nearly every psalm returns to the theme of praise
to God. That's the way the book of Psalms ends: "Let every thing that
hath breath praise the LORD. Praise ye the LORD" (150:6).

The psalmist David, a soldier and man of God, would have appreciated seeing these Israeli soldiers at prayer before the Western Wall of the temple.

QUOTABLE

- *O LORD our Lord, how excellent is thy name in all the earth! (8:1)*
- *The LORD is my shepherd; I shall not want. (23:1)*
- *Create in me a clean heart, O God; and renew a right spirit within me. (51:10)*
- *Thy word have I hid in mine heart, that I might not sin against thee. (119:11)*
- *I will lift up mine eyes unto the hills, from whence cometh my help. My help cometh from the LORD. (121:1–2)*

UNIQUE AND UNUSUAL

The book of Psalms is the Bible's longest, in terms of both number of chapters (150) and total word count. It contains the longest chapter in the Bible (Psalm 119, with 176 verses) and the shortest (Psalm 117, with 2 verses). Psalm 117 is also the midpoint of the Protestant Bible, with 594 chapters before it and 594 after.

SO WHAT?

The psalms run the gamut of human emotion—which is why so many people turn to them in times of both joy and sadness.

PROVERBS

Pithy, memorable sayings encourage
people to pursue wisdom.

AUTHORS / DATE

Primarily Solomon (1:1), with sections attributed to "the wise" (22:17), Agur (30:1), and King Lemuel (31:1). Little is known of the latter two. Solomon reigned approximately 970–930 BC. The staff of King Hezekiah, who lived about two hundred years later, "copied out" the latter chapters of the book we have today (25:1).

DETAILS, PLEASE

Proverbs doesn't have a story line—it's simply a collection of practical tips for living. Mainly from the pen of King Solomon, the wisest

In the most famous example of Solomon's wisdom, the king orders a baby boy cut in half to see which of the women claiming the child will sacrifice her claim to save her son.

human being ever (in 1 Kings 3:12 God said, "I have given thee a wise and an understanding heart; so that there was none like thee before thee, neither after thee shall any arise like unto thee"), the proverbs speak to issues such as work, money, sex, temptation, drinking, laziness, discipline, and child rearing. Underlying each proverb is the truth that "the fear of the LORD is the beginning of knowledge" (1:7).

QUOTABLE

- *Trust in the LORD with all thine heart; and lean not unto thine own understanding. (3:5)*
- *Go to the ant, thou sluggard; consider her ways, and be wise. (6:6)*
- *A wise son maketh a glad father: but a foolish son is the heaviness of his mother. (10:1)*
- *As a jewel of gold in a swine's snout, so is a fair woman which is without discretion. (11:22)*
- *He that spareth his rod hateth his son: but he that loveth him chasteneth him betimes. (13:24)*
- *A soft answer turneth away wrath: but grievous words stir up anger. (15:1)*
- *Commit thy works unto the LORD, and thy thoughts shall be established. (16:3)*
- *Even a fool, when he holdeth his peace, is counted wise. (17:28)*
- *The name of the LORD is a strong tower: the righteous runneth into it, and is safe. (18:10)*
- *Wine is a mocker, strong drink is raging. (20:1)*
- *A good name is rather to be chosen than great riches. (22:1)*
- *Answer not a fool according to his folly, lest thou also be like unto him. (26:4)*
- *Faithful are the wounds of a friend. (27:6)*

UNIQUE AND UNUSUAL

The final chapter of Proverbs—written by a little-known king named Lemuel—includes a long poem in praise of wives, rather unusual for that time and culture.

King Solomon had a particular fondness for wives—having married seven hundred women (1 Kings 11:3). But in his latter years they would prove less of a blessing, as some of them led him into idol worship.

SO WHAT?

Wisdom, as Proverbs 4:7 indicates, "is the principal thing. . .with all thy getting get understanding." If you need help with that, just ask God (James 1:5).

ECCLESIASTES

Apart from God, life is empty and unsatisfying.

AUTHOR / DATE

Not stated but probably Solomon. The author is identified as "the son of David" (1:1) and "king over Israel in Jerusalem" (1:12) and says he had "more wisdom than all they that have been before me" (1:16). Written around the 900s BC.

DETAILS, PLEASE

A king pursues the things of this world, only to find them unfulfilling. Learning, pleasure, work, laughter—"all is vanity" (1:2). The king also laments the inequities of life: people live, work hard, and die, only to leave their belongings to someone else; the wicked prosper over the righteous; the poor are oppressed. Nevertheless, the king realizes "the conclusion of the whole matter: Fear God, and keep his commandments: for this is the whole duty of man" (12:13).

QUOTABLE

- *I saw that wisdom excelleth folly, as far as light excelleth darkness. (2:13)*
- *To every thing there is a season, and a time to every purpose under the heaven. (3:1)*
- *Better is it that thou shouldest not vow, than that thou shouldest vow and not pay. (5:5)*
- *He that loveth silver shall not be satisfied with silver; nor he that loveth abundance with increase. (5:10)*
- *A good name is better than precious ointment. (7:1)*
- *Whatsoever thy hand findeth to do, do it with thy might. (9:10)*

- *Wisdom is better than weapons of war: but one sinner destroyeth much good. (9:18)*
- *Cast thy bread upon the waters: for thou shalt find it after many days. (11:1)*
- *Remember now thy Creator in the days of thy youth. (12:1)*

UNIQUE AND UNUSUAL

The book's generally negative tone makes some readers wonder if Solomon wrote it late in life, after his hundreds of wives led him to stray from God.

SO WHAT?

Life doesn't always make sense. . .but there's still a God who understands.

One oak in four seasons—the changing times of life form a recurring theme in the book of Ecclesiastes.

SONG OF SOLOMON

Married love is a beautiful thing worth celebrating.

AUTHOR / DATE

Solomon (1:1), though some wonder if the song "of Solomon" is like the psalms "of David"—which could mean they are *by, for,* or *about* him. Solomon ruled around 970–930 BC.

DETAILS, PLEASE

A dark-skinned beauty is marrying the king, and both are thrilled. "Behold, thou art fair, my love; behold, thou art fair; thou hast doves' eyes," he tells her (1:15). "Behold, thou art fair, my beloved, yea, pleasant: also our bed is green," she responds (1:16). Through eight chapters and 117 verses, the two lovers admire each other's physical beauty, expressing their love and devotion.

QUOTABLE

- *Let him kiss me with the kisses of his mouth: for thy love is better than wine. (1:2)*
- *He brought me to the banqueting house, and his banner over me was love. (2:4)*
- *Thy navel is like a round goblet, which wanteth not liquor: thy belly is like an heap of wheat set about with lilies. (7:2)*
- *Many waters cannot quench love, neither can the floods drown it. (8:7)*
- *Make haste, my beloved, and be thou like to a roe or to a young hart upon the mountains of spices. (8:14)*

UNIQUE AND UNUSUAL

Like the book of Esther, Song of Solomon never mentions the name "God."

SO WHAT?

God made marriage for the husband and wife's enjoyment—and that marital love can be a picture of God's joy in His people.

The man of the Song of Solomon described various parts of his lover's body as doves, towers, clusters of grapes, and fawns.

ISAIAH

A coming Messiah will save people from their sins.

AUTHOR / DATE

Isaiah, son of Amoz (1:1). Written around 740–700 BC, starting "in the year that king Uzziah died" (6:1).

DETAILS, PLEASE

Like most prophets, Isaiah announced the bad news of punishment for sin. But he also described a coming Messiah who would be "wounded for our transgressions. . .bruised for our iniquities. . .and with his stripes we are healed" (53:5). Called to the ministry through a stunning vision of God in heaven (chapter 6), Isaiah wrote a book that some call "the fifth Gospel" for its predictions of the birth, life, and death of Jesus Christ some seven hundred years later. These prophecies of redemption balance the depressing promises of God's discipline against Judah and Jerusalem, which were overrun by Babylonian armies about a century later. Isaiah's prophecy ends with a long section (chapters 40–66) describing God's restoration of Israel, His promised salvation, and His eternal kingdom.

QUOTABLE

- *Holy, holy, holy, is the Lord of hosts: the whole earth is full of his glory. (6:3)*
- *Behold, a virgin shall conceive, and bear a son, and shall call his name Immanuel. (7:14)*
- *For unto us a child is born, unto us a son is given: and the government shall be upon his shoulder: and his name shall be called Wonderful, Counsellor, The mighty God, The everlasting Father, The Prince of Peace. (9:6)*

- *All we like sheep have gone astray; we have turned every one to his own way; and the Lord hath laid on him the iniquity of us all. (53:6)*

Isaiah's lips are anointed with fire
by an angel so he would be better
able to spread God's word.

Isaiah had two children with strange, prophetic names. Shear-jashub (7:3) means "a remnant shall return," and Maher-shalal-hash-baz (8:3) means "haste to the spoil." Shear-jashub's name carried God's promise that exiled Jews would one day return home. Maher-shalal-hash-baz's name assured the king of Judah that his country's enemies would be handled by Assyrian armies.

SO WHAT?

Early in His ministry, Jesus said He fulfilled the prophecies of Isaiah: "The LORD hath anointed me to preach good tidings unto the meek; he hath sent me to bind up the brokenhearted, to proclaim liberty to the captives, and the opening of the prison to them that are bound; to proclaim the acceptable year of the LORD" (61:1–2). It's amazing how much God cares about us!

This Babylonian lion mosaic represented the fierceness of that country's leadership and armed forces.

JEREMIAH

After years of sinful behavior, Judah will be punished.

AUTHOR / DATE

Jeremiah (1:1), with the assistance of Baruch, a scribe (36:4). Written approximately 585 BC.

DETAILS, PLEASE

Called to the ministry as a boy (1:6), Jeremiah prophesies bad news to Judah: "Lo, I will bring a nation upon you from far, O house of Israel, saith the LORD" (5:15). Jeremiah is mocked for his prophecies, occasionally beaten, and imprisoned in a muddy well (chapter 38). But his words come true with the Babylonian invasion of chapter 52.

QUOTABLE

- *Before I formed thee in the belly I knew thee; and before thou camest forth out of the womb I sanctified thee. (1:5)*
- *Is there no balm in Gilead; is there no physician there? (8:22)*
- *Let him that glorieth glory in this, that he understandeth and knoweth me, that I am the LORD which exercise lovingkindness, judgment, and righteousness, in the earth. (9:24)*
- *Can the Ethiopian change his skin, or the leopard his spots? then may ye also do good, that are accustomed to do evil. (13:23)*
- *Behold, as the clay is in the potter's hand, so are ye in mine hand, O house of Israel. (18:6)*
- *Call unto me, and I will answer thee, and shew thee great and mighty things, which thou knowest not. (33:3)*

The burning of scrolls and books is an age-old tradition—but God's Word has always survived.

UNIQUE AND UNUSUAL

The book of Jeremiah that we read is apparently an expanded, second version of a destroyed first draft. King Jehoiakim, angry with Jeremiah for his dire prophecies, cut the scroll with a penknife and "cast it into the fire that was on the hearth" (36:23). At God's command, Jeremiah produced a second scroll with additional material (36:32).

SO WHAT?

Through Jeremiah, God gave Judah some forty years to repent. God "is longsuffering to us-ward, not willing that any should perish, but that all should come to repentance" (2 Peter 3:9).

LAMENTATIONS

A despairing poem about the destruction of Jerusalem.

AUTHOR / DATE

Not stated but traditionally attributed to Jeremiah. Probably written around 586 BC, shortly after the fall of Jerusalem to the Babylonians.

DETAILS, PLEASE

After warning the southern Jewish nation to obey God, the prophet Jeremiah witnesses the punishment he'd threatened. Judah's "enemies prosper; for the Lord hath afflicted her for the multitude of her transgressions," writes Jeremiah; "her children are gone into captivity before the enemy" (1:5). The sight brings tears to Jeremiah's eyes ("Mine eye runneth down with water," 1:16) and provides his nickname, "the weeping prophet." Lamentations ends with a plaintive cry: "Thou hast utterly rejected us; thou art very wroth against us" (5:22).

QUOTABLE

- *How doth the city sit solitary, that was full of people! how is she become as a widow! (1:1)*
- *For these things I weep; mine eye, mine eye runneth down with water, because the comforter that should relieve my soul is far from me. (1:16)*
- *He hath bent his bow, and set me as a mark for the arrow. (3:12)*
- *The Lord is my portion, saith my soul; therefore will I hope in him. (3:24)*
- *Turn thou us unto thee, O Lord, and we shall be turned; renew our days as of old. (5:21)*

UNIQUE AND UNUSUAL

Though Lamentations doesn't indicate its author, Jeremiah is described in 2 Chronicles as a composer of laments (35:25).

SO WHAT?

God's punishment might seem severe, but as the book of Hebrews says, "No chastening for the present seemeth to be joyous, but grievous: nevertheless afterward it yieldeth the peaceable fruit of righteousness unto them which are exercised thereby" (12:11).

The prophet Jeremiah sculpted on the giant menorah In front of the Israeli parliament.

EZEKIEL

Though Israel is in exile, the nation will be restored.

AUTHOR / DATE

Ezekiel, a priest (1:1–3). Written approximately the 590s–570s BC.

DETAILS, PLEASE

Ezekiel, an exiled Jew in Babylon, becomes God's spokesman to fellow exiles. He shares unusual (even bizarre) visions with the people, reminding them of the sin that led to their captivity but also offering hope of national restoration.

QUOTABLE

- *I have no pleasure in the death of him that dieth, saith the Lord GOD: wherefore turn yourselves, and live ye. (18:32)*
- *Thou art the anointed cherub. . . . Thou wast perfect in thy ways from the day that thou wast created, till iniquity was found in thee. (28:14–15)*
- *The name of the city from that day shall be, The LORD is there. (48:35)*

UNIQUE AND UNUSUAL

Ezekiel's vision of a valley of dry bones is one of the Bible's strangest images: "I prophesied as I was commanded: and. . .there was a noise, and behold a shaking, and the bones came together. . . . The sinews and the flesh came up upon them, and the skin covered them above. . . . And the breath came into them, and they lived, and stood up upon their feet, an exceeding great army" (37:7–8, 10).

SO WHAT?

Ezekiel strongly teaches personal responsibility: "The soul that sinneth, it shall die. But if a man be just, and do that which is lawful and right. . .he shall surely live" (18:4–5, 9).

The classic painter Raphael's depiction of Ezekiel's first vision.

DANIEL

Faithful to God in a challenging setting, Daniel is blessed.

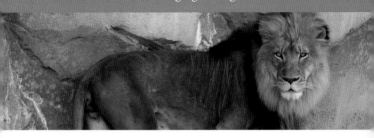

AUTHOR / DATE

Likely Daniel, though some question this. Chapters 7–12 are written in the first person ("I Daniel," 7:15), though the first six chapters are in the third person ("Then Daniel answered," 2:14). Probably written during the period of the Babylonian captivity, approximately 605–538 BC.

DETAILS, PLEASE

As a young man, Daniel—along with three others to be known as Shadrach, Meshach, and Abednego—is taken from his home in Jerusalem to serve the king of Babylon. Daniel's God-given ability to interpret dreams endears him to King Nebuchadnezzar, whose vision of a huge statue, Daniel says, represents existing and future kingdoms. Shadrach, Meshach, and Abednego find trouble when they disobey an order to bow before a statue of Nebuchadnezzar; as punishment, they are thrown into a fiery furnace, where they are protected by an angelic being "like the Son of God" (3:25). The next Babylonian king, Belshazzar, throws a drinking party using cups stolen from the temple in Jerusalem; he literally sees "the writing on the wall," which Daniel interprets as the soon-to-come takeover of Babylon by the Medes. The Median king, Darius, keeps Daniel as an adviser but is tricked into passing a law designed by other jealous officials to hurt Daniel, who ends up in a den of lions. Once again, God protects His people; Daniel spends a night in the den and remains unharmed, then is replaced by the schemers, who are mauled by the hungry beasts. The final six chapters contain Daniel's prophetic visions, including that of "seventy weeks" of the end times.

Shadrach, Meshach, and Abednego in the fiery furnace—
but still under the protection of the angel—in a nineteenth-
century painting by Simeon Solomon.

In this painting by Rubens, Daniel is seemingly in mortal danger. In actuality he is protected by earnest prayer.

QUOTABLE

- *Our God whom we serve is able to deliver us from the burning fiery furnace, and he will deliver us out of thine hand, O king. (3:17)*
- *My God hath sent his angel, and hath shut the lions' mouths, that they have not hurt me. (6:22)*
- *O my God. . .we do not present our supplications before thee for our righteousnesses, but for thy great mercies. (9:18)*

UNIQUE AND UNUSUAL

The book was originally written in two languages: Hebrew (the introduction and most of the prophecies, chapter 1 and chapters 8–12) and Aramaic (the stories of chapters 2–7).

SO WHAT?

As the old song says, "Dare to be a Daniel." God will always take care of the people who "dare to stand alone. . .to have a purpose firm" for Him.

HOSEA
Prophet's marriage to prostitute reflects
God's relationship with Israel.

AUTHOR / DATE

Probably Hosea himself, though the text is in both the first and the third person. Written sometime between 750 (approximately when Hosea began ministering) and 722 BC (when Assyria overran Israel).

DETAILS, PLEASE

God gives Hosea a strange command: "Take unto thee a wife of whoredoms" (1:2). The marriage pictures God's relationship to Israel—an honorable, loving husband paired with an unfaithful wife. Hosea marries an adulteress named Gomer and starts a family with her. When Gomer returns to her life of sin, Hosea—again picturing God's faithfulness—buys her back from the slave market. The book contains God's warnings for disobedience but also His promises of blessing for repentance.

QUOTABLE

- *My people are destroyed for lack of knowledge: because thou hast rejected knowledge, I will also reject thee. (4:6)*
- *I desired mercy, and not sacrifice; and the knowledge of God more than burnt offerings. (6:6)*
- *For they have sown the wind, and they shall reap the whirlwind. (8:7)*

UNIQUE AND UNUSUAL

Gomer had three children—perhaps Hosea's but maybe not—each given a prophetic name. Son Jezreel was named for a massacre, daughter Lo-ruhamah's name meant "not loved," and son Lo-ammi's name meant "not my people."

SO WHAT?

God is faithful, even when His people aren't—and He's always ready to forgive. "I will heal their backsliding," God said through Hosea; "I will love them freely" (14:4).

The artist James Joseph Jacques Tissot's impression of the prophet Hosea.

JOEL

Locust plague pictures God's judgment on His sinful people.

AUTHOR / DATE

Joel, son of Pethuel (1:1). Little else is known about him. Date of writing is unclear but possibly just before the Babylonian invasion of Judah in 586 BC.

DETAILS, PLEASE

A devastating locust swarm invades the nation of Judah, but Joel indicates this natural disaster is nothing compared to the coming "great and very terrible" day of the Lord (2:11). God plans to judge His people for sin, but they still have time to repent. Obedience will bring both physical and spiritual renewal: "I will pour out my spirit upon all flesh," God says (2:28). When the Holy Spirit comes on Christian believers at Pentecost, the apostle Peter quotes this passage to explain what has happened (Acts 2:17).

QUOTABLE

• *Whosoever shall call on the name of the LORD shall be delivered. (2:32)*

UNIQUE AND UNUSUAL

Unlike other prophets who condemned idolatry, injustice, or other specific sins of the Jewish people, Joel simply called for repentance without describing the sin committed.

SO WHAT?

Though God judges sin, He always offers a way out—in our time, through Jesus.

AMOS

Real religion isn't just ritual but treating people with justice.

AUTHOR / DATE

Amos, a shepherd from Tekoa, near Bethlehem (1:1). Written approximately the 760s BC.

DETAILS, PLEASE

An average guy—a lowly shepherd, actually—takes on the rich and powerful of Israelite society, condemning their idol worship, persecution of God's prophets, and cheating of the poor. Though God once rescued the people of Israel from slavery in Egypt, He is ready to send them into new bondage because of their sin. Amos sees visions that picture Israel's plight: a plumb line, indicating the people are not measuring up to God's standards, and a basket of ripe fruit, showing the nation is ripe for God's judgment.

QUOTABLE

- *Prepare to meet thy God, O Israel. (4:12)*
- *Let justice roll down as waters, and righteousness as a mighty stream. (5:24 ASV)*

UNIQUE AND UNUSUAL

A native of the southern Jewish kingdom of Judah, Amos was directed by God to prophesy in the northern Jewish nation of Israel.

SO WHAT?

How are you treating the people around you? In God's eyes, that's an indicator of your true spiritual condition. For a New Testament perspective, see James 2:14–18.

OBADIAH

Edom will suffer for participating in Jerusalem's destruction.

AUTHOR / DATE

Obadiah (1:1), perhaps a person by that name or an unnamed prophet for whom "Obadiah" (meaning "servant of God") is a title. Date of writing is unclear but probably within thirty years after Babylon's invasion of Judah in 586 BC.

DETAILS, PLEASE

Edom was a nation descended from Esau—twin brother of Jacob, the patriarch of Israel. The baby boys had struggled in their mother's womb (Genesis 25:21–26), and their conflict had continued over the centuries. After Edom took part in the Babylonian ransacking of Jerusalem, Obadiah passed down God's judgment: "For thy violence against thy brother Jacob shame shall cover thee, and thou shalt be cut off for ever" (1:10).

QUOTABLE

- *Upon mount Zion shall be deliverance. (1:17)*

UNIQUE AND UNUSUAL

Obadiah is the Old Testament's shortest book—only one chapter and twenty-one verses.

SO WHAT?

Obadiah shows God's faithfulness to His people. This prophecy is a fulfillment of God's promise from generations earlier: "I will bless them that bless thee, and curse him that curseth thee" (Genesis 12:3).

JONAH
Reluctant prophet, running from God,
is swallowed by giant fish.

AUTHOR / DATE

Unclear; the story is Jonah's but is written in the third person. Written approximately 760 BC. Jonah prophesied during the reign of Israel's King Jeroboam II (see 2 Kings 14:23–25), who ruled from about 793 to 753 BC.

DETAILS, PLEASE

God tells Jonah to preach repentance in Nineveh, capital of the brutal Assyrian Empire. Jonah disobeys, sailing in the opposite direction—toward a rendezvous with literary immortality. A storm rocks Jonah's ship, and he spends three days in a giant fish's belly before deciding to obey God after all. When Jonah preaches, Nineveh repents—and God spares the city from the destruction He'd threatened. But the prejudiced Jonah pouts. The story ends with God proclaiming His concern even for vicious pagans.

QUOTABLE

- *So they took up Jonah, and cast him forth into the sea: and the sea ceased from her raging. (1:15)*
- *Jonah was in the belly of the fish three days and three nights. (1:17)*
- *I will pay that that I have vowed. Salvation is of the LORD. (2:9)*
- *So the people of Nineveh believed God, and proclaimed a fast, and put on sackcloth, from the greatest of them even to the least of them. (3:5)*
- *Should not I spare Nineveh, that great city, wherein are more than sixscore thousand persons that cannot discern between their right hand and their left hand; and also much cattle? (4:11)*

UNIQUE AND UNUSUAL

Jonah's prophecy didn't come true—because of Nineveh's repentance.

SO WHAT?

God loves *everyone*—even the enemies of His chosen people. As Romans 5:8 says, "God commendeth his love toward us, in that, while we were yet sinners, Christ died for us."

In Michelangelo's painting on the ceiling of the Sistine Chapel in Rome, Jonah seems unaware of the approach of the giant fish.

MICAH

Israel and Judah will suffer for their idolatry and injustice.

AUTHOR / DATE

"The word of the Lord that came to Micah the Morasthite" (1:1). Micah either wrote the prophecies or dictated them to another. Written approximately 700 BC.

DETAILS, PLEASE

Micah chastises both the northern and southern Jewish nations for pursuing false gods and cheating the poor. The two nations will be devastated by invaders (the Assyrians), but God will preserve "the remnant of Israel" (2:12).

QUOTABLE

- *They shall beat their swords into plowshares, and their spears into pruninghooks: nation shall not lift up a sword against nation, neither shall they learn war any more. (4:3)*
- *He hath shewed thee, O man, what is good; and what doth the Lord require of thee, but to do justly, and to love mercy, and to walk humbly with thy God? (6:8)*
- *Who is a God like unto thee, that pardoneth iniquity, and passeth by the transgression of the remnant of his heritage? he retaineth not his anger for ever, because he delighteth in mercy. (7:18)*

Centuries before Jesus' birth, Micah predicted the town where it would occur: "But thou, Bethlehem Ephratah, though thou be little among the thousands of Judah, yet out of thee shall he come forth unto me that is to be ruler in Israel" (5:2).

A Christian church (left) and a Muslim mosque (tower at center) in modern Bethlehem.

SO WHAT?

Micah shows how God's judgment is tempered by mercy. "Who is a God like unto thee, that pardoneth iniquity, and passeth by the transgression of the remnant of his heritage? he retaineth not his anger for ever, because he delighteth in mercy" (7:18).

NAHUM

Powerful, wicked Nineveh will fall before God's judgment.

AUTHOR / DATE

"The book of the vision of Nahum the Elkoshite" (1:1). Nahum either wrote the prophecies or dictated them to another. Written sometime between 663 and 612 BC.

DETAILS, PLEASE

"Woe to the bloody city!" Nahum cries (3:1). Nineveh, capital of the brutal Assyrian Empire, has been targeted for judgment by God Himself, who will "make thee vile, and will set thee as a gazingstock" (3:6) for sins of idolatry and cruelty. Nahum's prophecy comes true when the Babylonian Empire overruns Nineveh in 612 BC.

QUOTABLE

- *The Lord is slow to anger. (1:3)*
- *The Lord is good, a strong hold in the day of trouble; and he knoweth them that trust in him. (1:7)*

UNIQUE AND UNUSUAL

Nahum is a kind of Jonah, part 2. Though the city had once avoided God's judgment by taking Jonah's preaching to heart and repenting, now, more than a century later, it will experience the full consequence of its sins.

SO WHAT?

Even the most powerful city on earth is no match for God's strength. Neither is the biggest problem in our individual lives.

HABAKKUK

Trust God even when He seems unresponsive or unfair.

AUTHOR / DATE

Habakkuk (1:1); nothing is known of his background. Written approximately 600 BC.

DETAILS, PLEASE

In Judah, a prophet complains that God allows violence and injustice among His people. But Habakkuk is shocked to learn the Lord's plan for dealing with the problem: sending the "bitter and hasty" (1:6) Chaldeans to punish Judah. Habakkuk argues that the Chaldeans are far worse than disobedient Jews. The Lord, however, says He's only using the Chaldeans for His purposes and will in time punish them for their own sins. It's not Habakkuk's job to question: "The LORD is in his holy temple: let all the earth keep silence before him" (2:20).

QUOTABLE

- *The just shall live by his faith. (2:4)*

UNIQUE AND UNUSUAL

The apostle Paul quotes Habakkuk 2:4 in his powerful gospel presentation in Romans 1.

SO WHAT?

Our world is much like Habakkuk's—full of violence and injustice—but God is still in control. Whether we sense it or not, He's working out His own purposes.

ZEPHANIAH

A coming "day of the Lord" promises heavy judgment.

AUTHOR / DATE

Zephaniah (1:1). Written approximately 640–620 BC, during the reign of King Josiah (1:1).

DETAILS, PLEASE

Zephaniah begins with a jarring prophecy: "I will utterly consume all things from off the land," God declares in the book's second verse. People, animals, birds, and fish will all perish, victims of God's wrath over Judah's idolatry. Other nearby nations will be punished, as well, in "the fire of my jealousy" (3:8), but there is hope: in His mercy, God will one day restore a remnant of Israel that "shall not do iniquity, nor speak lies" (3:13).

QUOTABLE

- *The great day of the LORD is near, it is near, and hasteth greatly. (1:14)*
- *Neither their silver nor their gold shall be able to deliver them in the day of the LORD's wrath. (1:18)*
- *Seek ye the LORD, all ye meek of the earth, which have wrought his judgment; seek righteousness, seek meekness: it may be ye shall be hid in the day of the LORD's anger. (2:3)*
- *The LORD will be terrible unto them: for he will famish all the gods of the earth; and men shall worship him, every one from his place, even all the isles of the heathen. (2:11)*
- *The LORD thy God in the midst of thee is mighty; he will save, he will rejoice over thee with joy. (3:17)*

UNIQUE AND UNUSUAL

Zephaniah gives more detail about himself than most of the minor prophets, identifying himself as a great-great-grandson of Hezekiah (1:1), probably the popular, godly king of Judah (2 Chronicles 29).

King Hezekiah, by an anonymous seventeenth-century Swedish artist.

SO WHAT?

God gave the people of Judah fair warning of His judgment, just as He has done with us. For Christians, the coming "day of the Lord" carries no fear.

HAGGAI

Jews returning from exile need to rebuild God's temple.

AUTHOR / DATE

Haggai (1:1). Written in 520 BC—a precise date because Haggai mentions "the second year of Darius the king" (1:1), which can be verified against Persian records.

DETAILS, PLEASE

One of three "postexilic" prophets, Haggai encourages former Babylonian captives to restore the demolished temple in Jerusalem. The new world power, Persia, has allowed the people to return to Jerusalem, but they've become distracted with building their own comfortable homes. Through Haggai, God tells the people to rebuild the temple first in order to break a drought that's affecting the countryside.

QUOTABLE

- *Now therefore thus saith the LORD of hosts; Consider your ways. (1:5)*
- *Ye have sown much, and bring in little; ye eat, but ye have not enough; ye drink, but ye are not filled with drink; ye clothe you, but there is none warm; and he that earneth wages earneth wages to put it into a bag with holes. (1:6)*
- *Be strong, all ye people of the land, saith the LORD, and work: for I am with you, saith the LORD of hosts. (2:4)*
- *I will shake all nations, and the desire of all nations shall come: and I will fill this house with glory, saith the LORD of hosts. (2:7)*

UNIQUE AND UNUSUAL

Haggai seems to hint at the end-times tribulation and second coming of Christ when he quotes God as saying, "I will shake the heavens, and the earth, and the sea, and the dry land; and I will shake all nations, and the desire of all nations shall come" (2:6–7).

SO WHAT?

Priorities are important. When we put God first, He is more inclined to bless us.

A nineteenth-century sketch of Darius, made from a rock relief found in modern-day Iran.

ZECHARIAH

Jewish exiles should rebuild their temple—
and anticipate their Messiah.

AUTHOR / DATE

Zechariah, son of Berechiah (1:1); some believe a second, unnamed
writer contributed chapters 9–14. Approximately 520–475 BC.

DETAILS, PLEASE

Like Haggai, another postexilic prophet, Zechariah urges Jewish
people to rebuild the Jerusalem temple. He also gives several prophecies of the coming Messiah, including an end-times vision of a final
battle over Jerusalem, when "the Lord [shall] go forth, and fight
against those nations. . . . And his feet shall stand in that day upon
the mount of Olives. . . . And the Lord shall be king over all the earth"
(14:3–4, 9).

QUOTABLE

- *Turn ye unto me, saith the Lord of hosts, and I will turn unto you, saith the Lord of hosts. (1:3)*
- *Behold a man riding upon a red horse, and he stood among the myrtle trees that were in the bottom. (1:8)*
- *Be silent, O all flesh, before the Lord: for he is raised up out of his holy habitation. (2:13)*
- *In those days it shall come to pass, that ten men shall take hold out of all languages of the nations, even shall take hold of the skirt of him that is a Jew, saying, We will go with you: for we have heard that God is with you. (8:23)*
- *In that day shall there be upon the bells of the horses, Holiness unto the Lord. (14:20)*

UNIQUE AND UNUSUAL

Zechariah's prophecy of the Messiah riding a donkey into Jerusalem (9:9) was fulfilled to the letter in Jesus' "triumphal entry" (Matthew 21:1–11). The prophecy "They shall look upon me whom they have pierced" (12:10) refers to the Roman soldiers' spearing of Christ after the crucifixion (John 19:34).

In the 1900 edition of the every-ten-years Oberammergau Passion Play, Anton Lang portrays Christ entering Jerusalem.

SO WHAT?

Knowing that many of Zechariah's specific prophecies were fulfilled in Jesus, we can trust that his other predictions—of the end times—will come true, too.

MALACHI

The Jews have become careless in their attitude toward God.

AUTHOR / DATE

Malachi (1:1), meaning "my messenger." No other details are given. Written approximately 450 BC.

DETAILS, PLEASE

Prophesying a century after the return from exile, Malachi chastises the Jews for offering "lame and sick" sacrifices (1:8); for divorcing their wives to marry pagan women (2:11, 14); and for failing to pay tithes for the temple (3:8). The Lord was angry with the attitude "It is vain to serve God" (3:14), but He promised to bless the obedient: "Unto you that fear my name shall the Sun of righteousness arise with healing in his wings" (4:2).

QUOTABLE

• *Return unto me, and I will return unto you, saith the Lord of hosts. (3:7)*

UNIQUE AND UNUSUAL

Malachi, the last book of the Old Testament, contains the final word from God for some four hundred years, until the appearance of John the Baptist and Jesus, the Messiah, as prophesied in Malachi 3:1: "I will send my messenger, and he shall prepare the way before me: and the Lord, whom ye seek, shall suddenly come to his temple."

SO WHAT?

God doesn't want empty religious rituals—He wants people to worship Him "in spirit and in truth" (John 4:24).

MATTHEW

Jesus fulfills the Old Testament
prophecies of a coming Messiah.

AUTHOR / DATE

Not stated but traditionally attributed to Matthew, a tax collector (9:9).
Matthew is also known as "Levi" (Mark 2:14). Written approximately
AD 70, when Romans destroyed the temple in Jerusalem.

DETAILS, PLEASE

The first of the four *Gospels* (meaning "good news"), the book of Matthew ties what follows in the New Testament to what came before
in the Old. The book, written primarily to a Jewish audience, uses
numerous Old Testament references to prove that Jesus is the promised Messiah the Jews have been anticipating for centuries. Beginning
with a genealogy that shows Jesus' ancestry through King David and
the patriarch Abraham, Matthew then details the angelic announce-
ment of Jesus' conception and the visit of the "wise men" with
their gifts of gold, frankincense, and myrrh. Matthew introduces
the character of John the Baptist, relative and forerunner of Jesus,
and describes the calling of key disciples Peter, Andrew, James, and
John. Jesus' teachings are emphasized, with long passages covering
His Sermon on the Mount (chapters 5–7), including the Beatitudes
("Blessed are they. . .") and the Lord's Prayer ("Our Father which art in
heaven. . ."). As with all four Gospels, Matthew also details the death,
burial, and resurrection of Jesus and is the only biographer of Jesus
to mention several miracles—the tearing of the temple curtain, an
earthquake, the breaking open of tombs, and the raising to life of
dead saints—that occurred during that time (27:50–54).

In many depictions of the Baptist, John holds a staff with a crosspiece signifying the preordained nature of the crucifixion.

QUOTABLE

- *She shall bring forth a son, and thou shalt call his name JESUS: for he shall save his people from their sins. (1:21)*
- *Ye are the salt of the earth. . . . Ye are the light of the world. (5:13–14)*
- *Love your enemies, bless them that curse you, do good to them that hate you, and pray for them which despitefully use you, and persecute you. (5:44)*

- *Judge not, that ye be not judged. (7:1)*
- *Ask, and it shall be given you; seek, and ye shall find; knock, and it shall be opened unto you. (7:7)*
- *Go ye therefore, and teach all nations, baptizing them in the name of the Father, and of the Son, and of the Holy Ghost. (28:19)*

UNIQUE AND UNUSUAL

Matthew is the only Gospel to use the terms "church" and "kingdom of heaven."

SO WHAT?

As Messiah, Jesus is also King—and worthy of our worship.

Jesus teaches His "Sermon on the Mount" in this nineteenth-century painting by Carl Bloch.

MARK

Jesus is God's Son, a suffering servant of all people.

AUTHOR / DATE

Not stated but traditionally attributed to John Mark, a missionary companion of Paul and Barnabas (Acts 12:25) and an associate of the apostle Peter (1 Peter 5:13). Probably written in the AD 60s, during the Roman persecution of Christians.

DETAILS, PLEASE

The second of the four Gospels is believed by most to be the first one written. The book of Mark is the briefest and most active of the four biographies of Jesus, the majority of which is repeated in the Gospels of Matthew and Luke. Mark addresses a Gentile audience, portraying Jesus as a man of action, divinely capable of healing the sick, controlling nature, and battling the powers of Satan. Mark's theme of the suffering servant comes through in his narratives of Jesus' interaction with hostile doubters—the Jewish leaders, who want to kill Him (9:31); His neighbors, who take offense at Him (6:3); and even His own family members, who think He's crazy (3:21). The abasement of Jesus pictures what His disciples should pursue: "Whosoever will be great among you, shall be your minister: and whosoever of you will be the chiefest, shall be servant of all. For even the Son of man came not to be ministered unto, but to minister, and to give his life a ransom for many" (10:43–45).

In the midst of the storm, some disciples try to control the boat and battle the waves—while others turn to Christ. The painting is by the Dutch master Rembrandt.

QUOTABLE

- *Come ye after me, and I will make you to become fishers of men. (1:17)*
- *Suffer the little children to come unto me, and forbid them not: for of such is the kingdom of God. (10:14)*
- *It is easier for a camel to go through the eye of a needle, than for a rich man to enter into the kingdom of God. (10:25)*
- *Render to Caesar the things that are Caesar's, and to God the things that are God's. (12:17)*
- *Watch ye and pray, lest ye enter into temptation. The spirit truly is ready, but the flesh is weak. (14:38)*

UNIQUE AND UNUSUAL

Many believe an unnamed spectator at Jesus' arrest, mentioned in Mark's Gospel, was Mark himself: "And there followed him a certain young man, having a linen cloth cast about his naked body; and the young men laid hold on him: and he left the linen cloth, and fled from them naked" (14:51–52).

In this woodcut from 1860, Judas kisses Jesus, soldiers arrest the Lord, Peter lashes out with his sword, and, behind Peter, a young man (still clothed) turns to run. Many believe this scared young man went on to write the original Gospel.

SO WHAT?

Suffering and loss aren't necessarily bad things—in fact, for Christians, they're the pathway to real life (8:35).

LUKE

Jesus is Savior of all people, whether Jew or Gentile.

AUTHOR / DATE

Not stated but traditionally attributed to Luke, a Gentile physician (Colossians 4:14) and a missionary companion of the apostle Paul (2 Timothy 4:11). Possibly written in the AD 70s–80s, as the Gospel was spreading throughout the Roman Empire.

DETAILS, PLEASE

Luke's Gospel is addressed to a man named Theophilus (1:3), "to set forth in order a declaration of those things which are most surely believed among us" about Jesus Christ (1:1). It's unclear who Theophilus was, though some believe he may have been a Roman official—and Luke's book is the least Jewish and most universal of the four Gospels. Luke traces Jesus' genealogy beyond Abraham, the patriarch of the Jews, all the way back to Adam, "the son of God" (3:38), common ancestor of everyone. Luke also shows Jesus' compassion for all people: Roman soldiers (7:1–10), widows (7:11–17), the "sinful" (7:36–50), the chronically ill (8:43–48), lepers (17:11–19), and many others—including a criminal condemned to die on a cross beside Jesus (23:40–43). As with all the Gospels, Luke shows Jesus' resurrection, adding detailed accounts of His appearances to two believers on the Emmaus road and the remaining eleven disciples. As the Gospel ends, Jesus is ascending into heaven—setting the stage for a sequel of sorts, Luke's book of Acts.

Jesus offers bread to His traveling companions in Emmaus. They had believed Him dead—only to discover Him traveling with them. This seventeenth-century painting is by an anonymous Italian artist.

QUOTABLE

- *And Mary said, My soul doth magnify the Lord, and my spirit hath rejoiced in God my Saviour. (1:46–47)*
- *Jesus answering said unto them, They that are whole need not a physician; but they that are sick. I came not to call the righteous, but sinners to repentance. (5:31–32)*
- *For where your treasure is, there will your heart be also. (12:34)*
- *I say unto you, that likewise joy shall be in heaven over one sinner that repenteth, more than over ninety and nine just persons, which need no repentance. (15:7)*

- *Whosoever shall seek to save his life shall lose it; and whosoever shall lose his life shall preserve it. (17:33)*
- *Whosoever shall not receive the kingdom of God as a little child shall in no wise enter therein. (18:17)*
- *For the Son of man is come to seek and to save that which was lost. (19:10)*

UNIQUE AND UNUSUAL

Luke is the only Gospel to share Jesus' stories ("parables") of the good Samaritan (10:25–37), the prodigal son (15:11–32), and the rich man and Lazarus (16:19–31). Luke is also the only Gospel to detail Jesus' actual birth and words He spoke in childhood (both in chapter 2).

SO WHAT?

It doesn't matter who you are, where you come from, or what you've done—Jesus came to seek and to save you.

A Roman centurion pleads with Jesus to heal his servant.
Stories like this showed Jesus as a Savior for all people.

JOHN

Jesus is God Himself, the only Savior of the world.

AUTHOR / DATE

Not stated but traditionally attributed to John, the "disciple whom Jesus loved" (John 21:7), brother of James and son of Zebedee (Matthew 4:21). Written around the AD 90s, as the last Gospel produced.

DETAILS, PLEASE

While the books of Matthew, Mark, and Luke have many similarities (they're called the "synoptic Gospels," meaning they take a common view), the book of John stands alone. The fourth Gospel downplays Jesus' parables (none are recorded) and miracles (only seven are featured). Instead, John provides more extensive treatments of Jesus' reasons for coming to earth ("I am come that they might have life, and that they might have it more abundantly," 10:10); His intimate relationship with God the Father ("I and my Father are one," 10:30); and His own feelings toward the job He had come to do ("Father, the hour is come; glorify thy Son, that thy Son also may glorify thee: as thou hast given him power over all flesh, that he should give eternal life to as many as thou hast given him," 17:1–2). John also gives special emphasis to Jesus' patient treatment of the disciples Thomas, who doubted the resurrection (20:24–29), and Peter, who had denied the Lord (21:15–23).

In this church fresco, God is portrayed as the Father, the crucified Son, and the Holy Spirit (as a dove).

QUOTABLE

- *In the beginning was the Word, and the Word was with God, and the Word was God. (1:1)*
- *For God so loved the world, that he gave his only begotten Son, that whosoever believeth in him should not perish, but have everlasting life. (3:16)*
- *I am the bread of life. (6:35)*
- *I am the good shepherd: the good shepherd giveth his life for the sheep. (10:11)*
- *I am the way, the truth, and the life: no man cometh unto the Father, but by me. (14:6)*

UNIQUE AND UNUSUAL

Jesus' very first miracle, His changing of water into wine at a wedding in Cana, is recorded only in John's Gospel (2:1–12). So are His raising of Lazarus from the dead (11:1–44), His healing of a man born blind (9:1–38), and His long-distance healing of a nobleman's son (4:46–54). John is also the only Gospel to mention Nicodemus, who heard Jesus' teaching that "ye must be born again" (3:7).

Still in his grave wrappings, Lazarus meets the friend who has become his personal Savior.

SO WHAT?

"These are written, that ye might believe that Jesus is the Christ, the Son of God; and that believing ye might have life through his name" (20:31).

ACTS

The Holy Spirit's arrival heralds the
beginning of the Christian church.

AUTHOR / DATE

Not stated but traditionally attributed to Luke, a Gentile physician
(Colossians 4:14), a missionary companion of the apostle Paul (2 Timothy 4:11), and the author of the Gospel of Luke. Covering events of
the AD 30s–60s, Acts was probably written sometime between AD 62
and 80.

DETAILS, PLEASE

Officially called "Acts of the Apostles," the book of Acts is a bridge
between the story of Jesus in the Gospels and the life of the church in
the letters that follow. Luke begins with Jesus' ascension into heaven
after forty days of post-resurrection activity, "speaking of the things
pertaining to the kingdom of God" (1:3). Ten days later, God sends
the Holy Spirit on the festival day of Pentecost—and the church is
born. Through the Spirit, the disciples are empowered to preach
boldly about Jesus, and three thousand people become Christians that
day. Jewish leaders, fearing the new movement called "this way" (9:2),
begin persecuting believers, who scatter to other areas and spread the
Gospel through much of the known world. The ultimate persecutor,
Saul, becomes a Christian himself after meeting the brightly shining,
heavenly Jesus on the road to Damascus. Saul, later called Paul, ultimately joins Peter and other Christian leaders in preaching, working
miracles, and strengthening the fledgling church.

The Holy Spirit rains down "tongues of fire" on Mary and the disciples.

QUOTABLE

- *Ye men of Galilee, why stand ye gazing up into heaven? this same Jesus, which is taken up from you into heaven, shall so come in like manner as ye have seen him go into heaven. (1:11)*
- *Repent, and be baptized every one of you in the name of Jesus Christ for the remission of sins, and ye shall receive the gift of the Holy Ghost. (2:38)*
- *Silver and gold have I none; but such as I have give I thee: In the name of Jesus Christ of Nazareth rise up and walk. (3:6)*
- *Neither is there salvation in any other: for there is none other name under heaven given among men, whereby we must be saved. (4:12)*
- *Whether it be right in the sight of God to hearken unto you more than unto God, judge ye. (4:19)*
- *And they stoned Stephen, calling upon God, and saying, Lord Jesus, receive my spirit. And he kneeled down, and cried with a loud voice, Lord, lay not this sin to their charge. And when he had said this, he fell asleep. (7:59–60)*
- *Saul, Saul, why persecutest thou me? (9:4)*

- *And the disciples were filled with joy, and with the Holy Ghost. (13:52)*
- *Sirs, what must I do to be saved? And they said, Believe on the Lord Jesus Christ, and thou shalt be saved, and thy house. (16:30–31)*

UNIQUE AND UNUSUAL

Acts tells of the first Christian martyr, Stephen, stoned to death for blaming Jewish leaders for the death of Jesus (chapter 7). Acts also depicts the Gospel's transition from a purely Jewish message to one for all people (9:15; 10:45) and the beginning of the Christian missionary movement (chapter 13).

SO WHAT?

Christians today are driven by the same force that Acts describes: "Ye shall receive power, after that the Holy Ghost is come upon you" (1:8).

A blinded Saul of Tarsus is cared for by Ananaias. His conversion (to Christianity and the new name "Paul") would enable the church to expand beyond the Holy Land.

ROMANS

Sinners are saved only by faith in Jesus Christ.

AUTHOR / DATE

The apostle Paul (1:1), with the secretarial assistance of Tertius (16:22). Written approximately AD 57, near the conclusion of Paul's third missionary journey.

DETAILS, PLEASE

Some call Romans a "theology textbook" for its thorough explanation of the Christian life. Paul begins by describing God's righteous anger against human sin (chapters 1–2), noting that everyone falls short of God's standard (3:23). But God Himself provides the only way to overcome that sin, "the righteousness of God which is by faith of Jesus Christ unto all and upon all them that believe" (3:22). Being justified (made right) through faith in Jesus, we can consider ourselves "to be dead indeed unto sin, but alive unto God through Jesus Christ our Lord" (6:11). God's Spirit will "quicken" (give life to, 8:11) all who believe in Jesus, allowing us to "present [our] bodies a living sacrifice, holy, acceptable unto God" (12:1). It is possible, with God's help, to "be not overcome of evil, but [to] overcome evil with good" (12:21).

QUOTABLE

- *All have sinned, and come short of the glory of God. (3:23)*
- *God commendeth his love toward us, in that, while we were yet sinners, Christ died for us. (5:8)*
- *The wages of sin is death; but the gift of God is eternal life through Jesus Christ our Lord. (6:23)*

- *O wretched man that I am! who shall deliver me from the body of this death? I thank God through Jesus Christ our Lord. (7:24–25)*
- *We know that all things work together for good to them that love God, to them who are the called according to his purpose. (8:28)*
- *Owe no man any thing, but to love one another: for he that loveth another hath fulfilled the law. (13:8)*
- *Love worketh no ill to his neighbour: therefore love is the fulfilling of the law. (13:10)*

Paul, writing one of his many letters of encouragement and education, in a painting from the sixteenth century.

UNIQUE AND UNUSUAL

Unlike Paul's other letters to churches, Romans was addressed to a congregation he'd never met. The great missionary was hoping to see the Roman Christians personally while traveling westward to Spain (15:23–24). It's unclear if Paul ever actually reached Spain or if he was executed in Rome after the end of the book of Acts.

SO WHAT?

In Paul's own words, "Therefore being justified by faith, we have peace with God through our Lord Jesus Christ" (5:1).

1 CORINTHIANS

An apostle tackles sin problems in the church at Corinth.

AUTHOR

The apostle Paul, with the assistance of Sosthenes (1:1). Written approximately AD 55–57.

DETAILS, PLEASE

Paul had helped found the church in Corinth (Acts 18) but then moved on to other mission fields. While in Ephesus, he learns of serious problems in the Corinthian congregation and writes a long letter to address those issues. For those arguing over who should lead the church, Paul urges "that ye be perfectly joined together in the same mind and in the same judgment" (1:10). For a man involved in an immoral relationship with his stepmother, Paul commands, "Put away from among yourselves that wicked person" (5:13). For those church members filing lawsuits against others, Paul warns, "Know ye not that the unrighteous shall not inherit the kingdom of God?" (6:9). The apostle also teaches on marriage, Christian liberty, the Lord's Supper, spiritual gifts, and the resurrection of the dead. In the famous thirteenth chapter of 1 Corinthians, Paul describes the "more excellent way" (12:31): that of charity, or love.

QUOTABLE

- *For the preaching of the cross is to them that perish foolishness; but unto us which are saved it is the power of God. (1:18)*
- *The foolishness of God is wiser than men; and the weakness of God is stronger than men. (1:25)*
- *For other foundation can no man lay than that is laid, which is Jesus Christ. (3:11)*

- *Take heed lest by any means this liberty of yours become a stumblingblock to them that are weak. (8:9)*
- *I am made all things to all men, that I might by all means save some. (9:22)*
- *For as often as ye eat this bread, and drink this cup, ye do shew the Lord's death till he come. (11:26)*
- *Though I speak with the tongues of men and of angels, and have not charity, I am become as sounding brass, or a tinkling cymbal. (13:1)*

While the Temple of Apollo at Corinth lies in ruins today, the faith that was preached to the Corinthian Christians is alive and well.

UNIQUE AND UNUSUAL

Refuting opponents who questioned his apostleship, Paul insists that he is as much an apostle as Jesus' original disciples. "Am I not an apostle?" he asks in 1 Corinthians 9:1. "Have I not seen Jesus Christ our Lord?"

SO WHAT?

Church problems are nothing new—neither is the way to correct them. Personal purity, self-discipline, and love for others are vital to a congregation's success.

2 CORINTHIANS

Paul defends his ministry to the troubled Corinthian church.

AUTHOR / DATE

The apostle Paul, with Timothy's assistance (1:1). Written approximately AD 55–57, shortly after the writing of 1 Corinthians.

DETAILS, PLEASE

Corinthian believers had apparently addressed some of the problems Paul's first letter mentioned—though there were still troublemakers who questioned his authority. He was forced to "speak foolishly" (11:21), boasting of hardships he'd faced serving Jesus: "in labours more abundant, in stripes above measure, in prisons more frequent, in deaths oft" (11:23). Paul even suffered a "thorn in the flesh" (12:7), which God refused to take away, telling him instead, "My grace is sufficient for thee: for my strength is made perfect in weakness" (12:9). His parting warning: "Examine yourselves, whether ye be in the faith; prove your own selves" (13:5).

QUOTABLE

- *For as the sufferings of Christ abound in us, so our consolation also aboundeth by Christ. (1:5)*
- *Now thanks be unto God, which always causeth us to triumph in Christ. (2:14)*
- *Therefore if any man be in Christ, he is a new creature: old things are passed away; behold, all things are become new. (5:17)*
- *For he hath made him to be sin for us, who knew no sin; that we might be made the righteousness of God in him. (5:21)*

- *And no marvel; for Satan himself is transformed into an angel of light. (11:14)*
- *Examine yourselves, whether ye be in the faith; prove your own selves. (13:5)*

UNIQUE AND UNUSUAL

Paul never identifies his "thorn in the flesh," though some speculate it may have been bad eyesight, temptations, even physical unattractiveness.

SO WHAT?

Christians should respect authority—whether in the church, the home, or society at large.

Paul wrote to prove his credentials to the Corinthians, listing the sufferings he had experienced for Christ—including surviving three shipwrecks.

GALATIANS

Christians are free from restrictive Jewish laws.

AUTHOR / DATE

The apostle Paul (1:1). Perhaps written around AD 49, as one of Paul's earliest letters.

DETAILS, PLEASE

Writing to several regional churches, Paul can only "marvel" (1:6) that Galatian Christians have turned from their freedom in Jesus back to the rules of Old Testament Judaism. Some people tried to compel Christians "to live as do the Jews" (2:14), an error even the apostle Peter made (2:11–13). Paul argued strongly "that no man is justified by the law in the sight of God. . .for, The just shall live by faith" (3:11).

QUOTABLE

- *But though we, or an angel from heaven, preach any other gospel unto you than that which we have preached unto you, let him be accursed. (1:8)*
- *I am crucified with Christ: nevertheless I live; yet not I, but Christ liveth in me. (2:20)*
- *O foolish Galatians, who hath bewitched you, that ye should not obey the truth? (3:1)*
- *For ye are all the children of God by faith in Christ Jesus. (3:26)*
- *But the fruit of the Spirit is love, joy, peace, longsuffering, gentleness, goodness, faith, meekness, temperance: against such there is no law. (5:22–23)*

One of Paul's closing comments, "Ye see how large a letter I have written unto you with mine own hand" (6:11), makes some believe that poor eyesight was the apostle's "thorn in the flesh" (2 Corinthians 12:7).

SO WHAT?

Old Testament rules don't control Christians' lives—but God's Spirit should: "Walk in the Spirit, and ye shall not fulfil the lust of the flesh" (5:16).

While the cross and the star of David may work well together in decorative architecture, for the new Christian church submitting to Jewish customs and rules was a retrograde step.

EPHESIANS

Christians are all members of Jesus' "body," the church.

AUTHOR / DATE

The apostle Paul (1:1). Written around AD 62, toward the end of Paul's life.

DETAILS, PLEASE

Paul had started the church in Ephesus (Acts 19) and now explains in detail the church members' relationship to Jesus Christ—so that they "may grow up into him in all things, which is the head, even Christ" (4:15). Through Jesus, God has reconciled both Jews and Gentiles to Himself (2:11–18). This new life should result in pure, honest living in the church and in the home (chapters 4–6).

QUOTABLE

- *For by grace are ye saved through faith; and that not of yourselves: it is the gift of God: not of works, lest any man should boast. (2:8–9)*
- *There is one body, and one Spirit, even as ye are called in one hope of your calling; one Lord, one faith, one baptism, one God and Father of all, who is above all, and through all, and in you all. (4:4–6)*
- *Be ye kind one to another, tenderhearted, forgiving one another, even as God for Christ's sake hath forgiven you. (4:32)*
- *Be not drunk with wine, wherein is excess; but be filled with the Spirit. (5:18)*
- *Husbands, love your wives, even as Christ also loved the church, and gave himself for it. (5:25)*
- *Put on the whole armour of God, that ye may be able to stand against the wiles of the devil. (6:11)*

UNIQUE AND UNUSUAL

Paul tells servants (slaves, in today's language) to "be obedient to them that are your masters" (6:5). Why? Because God will reward such behavior (6:8).

SO WHAT?

"In him [Jesus] you too are being built together to become a dwelling in which God lives by his Spirit" (2:22 NIV).

Just as babies grow and are influenced by their parents, so young Christians should move forward, following the example of their Father in heaven.

PHILIPPIANS

"Friendship letter" between the
apostle Paul and a beloved church.

AUTHOR / DATE

The apostle Paul, along with Timothy (1:1). Probably written in the early 60s AD.

DETAILS, PLEASE

With sixteen references to "joy" and "rejoicing," Philippians is one of the apostle Paul's most upbeat letters—even though he wrote it in "bonds" (1:13). Paul thanks the church at Philippi for its support (1:5) and encourages its people to "rejoice in the Lord alway: and again I say, Rejoice" (4:4).

QUOTABLE

- *For to me to live is Christ, and to die is gain. (1:21)*
- *At the name of Jesus every knee should bow, of things in heaven, and things in earth, and things under the earth; and that every tongue should confess that Jesus Christ is Lord, to the glory of God the Father. (2:10–11)*
- *What things were gain to me, those I counted loss for Christ. (3:7)*
- *I press toward the mark for the prize of the high calling of God in Christ Jesus. (3:14)*
- *Be careful for nothing; but in every thing by prayer and supplication with thanksgiving let your requests be made known unto God. (4:6)*
- *Whatsoever things are true, whatsoever things are honest, whatsoever things are just, whatsoever things are pure, whatsoever things are lovely, whatsoever things are of good report; if there be any virtue, and if there be any praise, think on these things. (4:8)*

Despite being blinded, mocked, imprisoned, shipwrecked, even bitten by a snake during his missionary work, the apostle Paul's overriding attitude remained one of joy that Jesus had saved him.

UNIQUE AND UNUSUAL

Though unity is a common theme in Paul's letters, he singles out two Philippian women, Euodias and Syntyche, pleading that they "be of the same mind in the Lord" (4:2).

SO WHAT?

When we live in the joy of the Lord, "the peace of God, which passeth all understanding, shall keep [our] hearts and minds through Christ Jesus" (4:7).

COLOSSIANS

Jesus Christ is supreme—over everyone and everything.

AUTHOR / DATE

The apostle Paul, along with Timothy (1:1). Probably written in the early 60s AD.

DETAILS, PLEASE

False teaching ("enticing words," 2:4) had infiltrated the church at Colosse, apparently causing some people to add unnecessary and unhelpful elements to their Christian faith. Paul sent this letter to remind Christians of the superiority of Jesus over Jewish rules and regulations (2:16), angels (2:18), and anything else. Jesus is "the image of the invisible God, the firstborn of every creature" (1:15).

QUOTABLE

- *For this cause we also, since the day we heard it, do not cease to pray for you. (1:9)*
- *Beware lest any man spoil you through philosophy and vain deceit, after the tradition of men, after the rudiments of the world, and not after Christ. (2:8)*
- *Set your affection on things above, not on things on the earth. (3:2)*
- *Let the peace of God rule in your hearts, to the which also ye are called in one body; and be ye thankful. (3:15)*
- *Fathers, provoke not your children to anger, lest they be discouraged. (3:21)*
- *Let your speech be always with grace, seasoned with salt, that ye may know how ye ought to answer every man. (4:6)*

UNIQUE AND UNUSUAL

Paul mentions a letter to Laodicea (4:16) that apparently did not make the cut as New Testament scripture.

We don't know how many of Paul's letters went astray. What we do know is that God preserved the ones He wanted His children to read.

SO WHAT?

"Beware lest any man spoil you through philosophy and vain deceit, after the tradition of men. . .and not after Christ" (2:8).

1 THESSALONIANS

Jesus will return to gather His followers to Him.

AUTHOR / DATE

The apostle Paul, along with Silvanus (Silas) and Timothy (1:1). Written around the early 50s AD—perhaps Paul's earliest letter.

DETAILS, PLEASE

In this letter to another church he helped found (see Acts 17), Paul teaches on the second coming of Christ, apparently an issue of some concern to the Thessalonians. Paul describes *how* Jesus will return but doesn't say exactly *when*. The important thing, in his words, is "that ye would walk worthy of God, who hath called you unto his kingdom and glory" (2:12).

QUOTABLE

- *For the Lord himself shall descend from heaven with a shout, with the voice of the archangel, and with the trump of God: and the dead in Christ shall rise first. (4:16)*
- *The day of the Lord so cometh as a thief in the night. (5:2)*

UNIQUE AND UNUSUAL

First Thessalonians contains two of the Bible's shortest verses: "Rejoice evermore" (5:16) and "Pray without ceasing" (5:17).

SO WHAT?

The Thessalonians were told to live right in view of Jesus' coming return. With the passage of two thousand years, don't you think it's even more important for us today?

The Thessalonians may have been overanxious, but today the message of the Lord's return is often mocked or simply ignored.

2 THESSALONIANS

Christians should work until Jesus returns.

AUTHOR / DATE

The apostle Paul, along with Silvanus (Silas) and Timothy (1:1). Written around the early 50s AD—perhaps Paul's second-oldest letter.

DETAILS, PLEASE

Shortly after writing 1 Thessalonians, Paul dictates a follow-up. Apparently, a letter falsely claiming to be from Paul had left the Thessalonians "shaken in mind. . .troubled" (2:2) at the thought that Jesus had already returned. Paul assures them that the event is still future—and urges everyone to live positive and productive lives until the second coming. "If any would not work," Paul commands those who have dropped out in anticipation of Jesus' return, "neither should he eat" (3:10).

QUOTABLE

- *You who are troubled rest with us, when the Lord Jesus shall be revealed from heaven with his mighty angels. (1:7)*
- *Brethren, be not weary in well doing. (3:13)*

UNIQUE AND UNUSUAL

The fact that Paul dictated this letter is clear from his comment "The salutation of Paul with mine own hand. . .so I write" (3:17).

SO WHAT?

As with all of the Christian life, balance is key: We should always look forward to Jesus' return, but we should also be busy doing good while we're here on earth.

1 TIMOTHY

Pastors are taught how to conduct their lives and churches.

AUTHOR / DATE

The apostle Paul (1:1). Written approximately AD 63.

DETAILS, PLEASE

The first of three "pastoral epistles," 1 Timothy contains the aging apostle Paul's insights for a new generation of church leaders. Timothy had often worked alongside Paul but was now pastoring in Ephesus (1:3). Paul warned him against legalism and false teaching (chapter 1), listed the qualifications for pastors and deacons (chapter 3), and described the behavior of a "good minister of Jesus Christ" (4:6) in the final three chapters.

QUOTABLE

- *This is a faithful saying, and worthy of all acceptation, that Christ Jesus came into the world to save sinners; of whom I am chief. (1:15)*
- *This is good and acceptable in the sight of God our Saviour; who will have all men to be saved, and to come unto the knowledge of the truth. (2:3–4)*
- *There is one God, and one mediator between God and men, the man Christ Jesus. (2:5)*
- *This is a true saying, if a man desire the office of a bishop, he desireth a good work. (3:1)*
- *Refuse profane and old wives' fables, and exercise thyself rather unto godliness. (4:7)*
- *We brought nothing into this world, and it is certain we can carry nothing out. (6:7)*

UNIQUE AND UNUSUAL

First Timothy seems to command good pay for pastors: "Let the elders that rule well be counted worthy of double honour.... The labourer is worthy of his reward" (5:17–18).

SO WHAT?

Though 1 Timothy is a letter to a pastor, Paul's teaching "that thou mayest know how thou oughtest to behave thyself in the house of God" (3:15) can speak to the rest of us, too.

Teachers guide young students in the classroom. The apostle Paul was just as diligent in explaining the truth of the Gospel to the next generation.

2 TIMOTHY

The apostle Paul's final words to a beloved coworker.

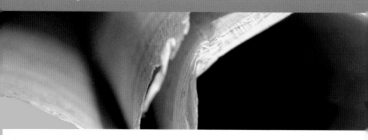

AUTHOR / DATE

The apostle Paul (1:1). Probably written in the mid-60s AD.

DETAILS, PLEASE

Second Timothy may be the last known letter of Paul. Addressed to "Timothy, my dearly beloved son" (1:2), the book warns the young pastor against false teaching and urges him to live a life of purity before his congregation. Timothy should expect trouble ("All that will live godly in Christ Jesus shall suffer persecution," 3:12), but God will be faithful ("The Lord shall deliver me from every evil work, and will preserve me unto his heavenly kingdom," 4:18). Paul begs Timothy to join him as quickly as possible, as "the time of my departure is at hand" (4:6).

QUOTABLE

- *Thou therefore endure hardness, as a good soldier of Jesus Christ. (2:3)*

UNIQUE AND UNUSUAL

Paul tells where the Bible comes from in 2 Timothy: "All scripture is given by inspiration of God" (3:16). The idea of the word *inspiration* is "breathed out."

SO WHAT?

We should all live life in such a way that we can say, like Paul, "I have fought a good fight, I have finished my course, I have kept the faith" (4:7).

TITUS

Church leaders are instructed on their lives and teaching.

AUTHOR / DATE

The apostle Paul (1:1). Written approximately AD 63.

DETAILS, PLEASE

On the Mediterranean island of Crete, Paul left Titus to "set in order the things that are wanting, and ordain elders" (1:5) for the fledgling church. Known for their poor behavior (see "Unique and Unusual" on page 124), the people of Crete needed the kind of church leader who would hold fast to "the faithful word as he hath been taught, that he may be able by sound doctrine both to exhort and to convince the gainsayers" (1:9).

QUOTABLE

- *Unto the pure all things are pure: but unto them that are defiled and unbelieving is nothing pure. (1:15)*
- *Speak thou the things which become sound doctrine. (2:1)*
- *Looking for that blessed hope, and the glorious appearing of the great God and our Saviour Jesus Christ. (2:13)*
- *Let no man despise thee. (2:15)*
- *Not by works of righteousness which we have done, but according to his mercy he saved us, by the washing of regeneration, and renewing of the Holy Ghost. (3:5)*

UNIQUE AND UNUSUAL

Paul quotes a Cretan philosopher in this letter: "One of themselves, even a prophet of their own, said, The Cretians are alway liars, evil beasts, slow bellies" (1:12). The quotation is from Epimenides, of the sixth century BC.

SO WHAT?

Though church leaders are held to a high standard, so are the people in the pews. What's good for the pastor is good for everyone else.

The mythical Minotaur—half man, half bull—was said to come from the island of Crete.

PHILEMON

Paul begs mercy for a runaway
slave converted to Christianity.

AUTHOR / DATE

The apostle Paul (1:1). Probably written around AD 63, when Paul was
imprisoned in Rome.

DETAILS, PLEASE

Philemon is a "fellowlabourer" (1:1) of Paul, a man who has
"refreshed" (1:7) other Christians with his love and generosity. But
the apostle writes with a deeper request—that Philemon forgive and
take back a runaway slave, who apparently accepted Christ under
Paul's teaching: "my son Onesimus, whom I have begotten in my
bonds" (1:10). "If thou count me therefore a partner," Paul wrote to
Philemon, "receive him as myself" (1:17).

QUOTABLE

- *I thank my God, making mention of thee always in my prayers, hearing of
  thy love and faith, which thou hast toward the Lord Jesus, and toward all
  saints. (1:4–5)*
- *If thou count me therefore a partner, receive him as myself. (1:17)*
- *Having confidence in thy obedience I wrote unto thee, knowing that thou
  wilt also do more than I say. (1:21)*
- *The grace of our Lord Jesus Christ be with your spirit. Amen. (1:25)*

UNIQUE AND UNUSUAL

With only one chapter and twenty-five verses, Philemon is the short-est of Paul's letters in the Bible.

SO WHAT?

Christians are called to forgive, and here's a practical example to con-sider. With God's help, will you let go of your grudges?

$100 REWARD !

Ranaway from Richards' Ferry, Culpe-per County, Va., 23rd instant, ABRAM, who is about 30 years old, 5 feet from 8 to 10 inches high, and weighs from 175 to 180. His complexion is dark, though not black, and hair long for a negro. He is a very shrewd fellow, and there is reason to believe he is attempting to get to a free State. I will give the above Reward if ta-ken out of Virginia—$50 if taken 20 miles from home, or $20 if taken in the neigh-borhood.   WM. T. J. RICHARDS,
        Adm'r of Jas. Richards, Dec'd.
    Sept. 24.

Many runaway slaves were returned to their owners in chains, for monetary rewards. Paul asked Philemon to take Onesimus back for love, as a brother in Christ.

HEBREWS

Jesus is better than any Old Testament person or sacrifice.

AUTHOR / DATE

Not stated; Paul, Luke, Barnabas, and Apollos have all been suggested. Probably written sometime before AD 70, since Hebrews refers to temple sacrifices. The Jerusalem temple was destroyed by Romans in AD 70.

DETAILS, PLEASE

Written to Jewish Christians (hence the name "Hebrews"), this long letter emphasizes the superiority of Christianity to Old Testament Judaism. Jesus is "so much better" (1:4) than angels, Moses, and the previous animal sacrifices. "For if the blood of bulls and of goats, and the ashes of an heifer sprinkling the unclean, sanctifieth to the purifying of the flesh," Hebrews asks, "how much more shall the blood of Christ, who through the eternal Spirit offered himself without spot to God, purge your conscience from dead works to serve the living God?" (9:13–14). Jewish Christians, some of whom were apparently wavering in their commitment to Jesus, are reminded that Christ "is the mediator of a better covenant, which was established upon better promises" (8:6)—a once-for-all sacrifice on the cross that provides "eternal redemption for us" (9:12).

QUOTABLE

- *How shall we escape, if we neglect so great salvation. (2:3)*
- *There remaineth therefore a rest to the people of God. (4:9)*
- *It is appointed unto men once to die, but after this the judgment. (9:27)*

- *Not forsaking the assembling of ourselves together, as the manner of some is; but exhorting one another: and so much the more, as ye see the day approaching. (10:25)*
- *Now faith is the substance of things hoped for, the evidence of things not seen. (11:1)*
- *Wherefore seeing we also are compassed about with so great a cloud of witnesses, let us lay aside every weight, and the sin which doth so easily beset us, and let us run with patience the race that is set before us, looking unto Jesus the author and finisher of our faith. (12:1–2)*
- *Let brotherly love continue. (13:1)*

Even the angel cries in Edouard Manet's depiction of the the body of Christ, the ultimate sacrifice.

UNIQUE AND UNUSUAL

Hebrews is one of only two New Testament letters (the other being 1 John) that includes no greeting or hint of its author.

SO WHAT?

"Having therefore, brethren, boldness to enter into the holiest by the blood of Jesus. . .let us draw near with a true heart in full assurance of faith, having our hearts sprinkled from an evil conscience, and our bodies washed with pure water" (10:19, 22).

Olympic athlete and missionary Eric Liddell was a prime example of one who ran the race that was set before him. He surely found Jesus at his last finishing tape.

JAMES

Real Christian faith is shown by one's good works.

AUTHOR / DATE

James (1:1), probably a half-brother of Jesus (see Matthew 13:55; Mark 6:3). Written approximately AD 60.

DETAILS, PLEASE

Though the apostle Paul clearly taught that salvation is by faith alone and not by good works (see Romans 3:28), James clarifies that good works will *follow* true faith: "What doth it profit, my brethren, though a man say he hath faith, and have not works?" (2:14). James encourages Christians, in everyday life, to view trials as opportunities for spiritual growth, to control their tongues, to make peace, to avoid favoritism, and to help the needy. The bottom line? "Therefore to him that knoweth to do good, and doeth it not, to him it is sin" (4:17).

QUOTABLE

- *If any of you lack wisdom, let him ask of God, that giveth to all men liberally, and upbraideth not; and it shall be given him. (1:5)*
- *A double minded man is unstable in all his ways. (1:8)*
- *Let no man say when he is tempted, I am tempted of God: for God cannot be tempted with evil, neither tempteth he any man: but every man is tempted, when he is drawn away of his own lust, and enticed. (1:13–14)*
- *Pure religion and undefiled before God and the Father is this, To visit the fatherless and widows in their affliction, and to keep himself unspotted from the world. (1:27)*

- *Whosoever shall keep the whole law, and yet offend in one point, he is guilty of all. (2:10)*
- *Even so faith, if it hath not works, is dead, being alone. (2:17)*
- *Ye ask, and receive not, because ye ask amiss, that ye may consume it upon your lusts. (4:3)*
- *Draw nigh to God, and he will draw nigh to you. (4:8)*
- *Ye ought to say, If the Lord will, we shall live, and do this, or that. (4:15)*
- *The effectual fervent prayer of a righteous man availeth much. (5:16)*
- *He which converteth the sinner from the error of his way shall save a soul from death, and shall hide a multitude of sins. (5:20)*

UNIQUE AND UNUSUAL

For those who think it's enough just to believe in God, James says, "The devils also believe, and tremble" (2:19). Life-changing faith in Jesus is the key.

SO WHAT?

Want practical wisdom for living the Christian life? You'll find it all through the book of James.

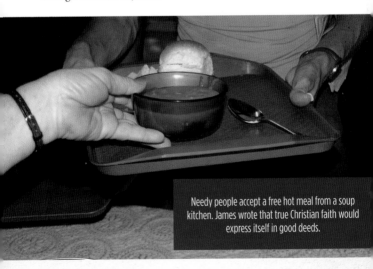

Needy people accept a free hot meal from a soup kitchen. James wrote that true Christian faith would express itself in good deeds.

1 PETER

Suffering for the sake of Jesus is noble and good.

AUTHOR / DATE

The apostle Peter (1:1), with the assistance of Silvanus (Silas, 5:12). Written approximately AD 65.

DETAILS, PLEASE

As the early church grows, the Roman Empire begins persecuting Christians—and Peter assures them that God is still in control: "Beloved, think it not strange concerning the fiery trial which is to try you, as though some strange thing happened unto you" (4:12). What is the proper response to such suffering? "Rejoice, inasmuch as ye are partakers of Christ's sufferings; that, when his glory shall be revealed, ye may be glad also with exceeding joy" (4:13).

QUOTABLE

- As he which hath called you is holy, so be ye holy in all manner of conversation. (1:15)
- All flesh is as grass, and all the glory of man as the flower of grass. The grass withereth, and the flower thereof falleth away: but the word of the Lord endureth for ever. (1:24–25)
- Not rendering evil for evil, or railing for railing: but contrariwise blessing; knowing that ye are thereunto called, that ye should inherit a blessing. (3:9)
- If any man suffer as a Christian, let him not be ashamed; but let him glorify God on this behalf. (4:16)
- Be sober, be vigilant; because your adversary the devil, as a roaring lion, walketh about, seeking whom he may devour. (5:8)

The eight members of Noah's family leave the ark in a Bible illustration from 1860.

UNIQUE AND UNUSUAL

Peter clarifies exactly how many people rode out the great flood on Noah's ark: eight (3:20). Genesis indicates that "Noah. . .and his sons, and his wife, and his sons' wives" (Genesis 7:7) were in the boat but leaves unsaid whether any sons might have had multiple wives.

SO WHAT?

Life may be hard, but God is always good. And for Christians, there's a much better day ahead.

2 PETER

Beware of false teachers within the church.

AUTHOR / DATE

The apostle Peter (1:1). Probably written in the late 60s AD, shortly before Peter's execution.

DETAILS, PLEASE

The Christian qualities of faith, virtue, knowledge, self-control, patience, godliness, and love (1:5–8), coupled with a reliance on scripture (1:19–21), will help believers avoid the false teachings of those who "privily shall bring in damnable heresies, even denying the Lord that bought them" (2:1).

QUOTABLE

- *We have not followed cunningly devised fables, when we made known unto you the power and coming of our Lord Jesus Christ, but were eyewitnesses of his majesty. (1:16)*
- *Prophecy came not in old time by the will of man: but holy men of God spake as they were moved by the Holy Ghost. (1:21)*
- *The Lord is not slack concerning his promise, as some men count slackness; but is longsuffering to us-ward, not willing that any should perish, but that all should come to repentance. (3:9)*
- *Grow in grace, and in the knowledge of our Lord and Saviour Jesus Christ. (3:18)*

UNIQUE AND UNUSUAL

Peter wrote this letter knowing his death was near: "Shortly I must put off this my tabernacle, even as our Lord Jesus Christ hath shewed me" (1:14).

SO WHAT?

"Beware lest ye also, being led away with the error of the wicked, fall from your own stedfastness" (3:17).

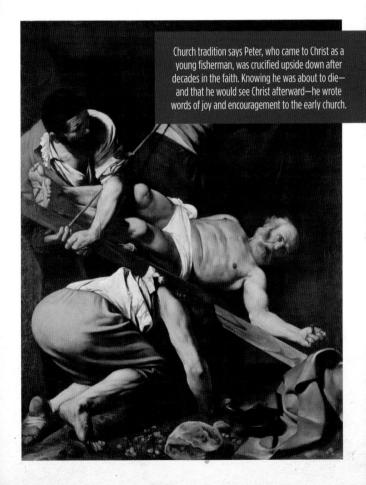

Church tradition says Peter, who came to Christ as a young fisherman, was crucified upside down after decades in the faith. Knowing he was about to die—and that he would see Christ afterward—he wrote words of joy and encouragement to the early church.

1 JOHN

Jesus was real man just as He is real God.

AUTHOR / DATE

Not stated but according to church tradition, the apostle John. Written approximately AD 92.

DETAILS, PLEASE

First John tackles a strange heresy that claimed Jesus had been on earth only in spirit, not in body: "Every spirit that confesseth not that Jesus Christ is come in the flesh is not of God: and this is that spirit of antichrist" (4:3). John wrote that he knew Jesus personally, as one "which we have looked upon, and our hands have handled" (1:1), and that knowledge leads to a saving belief in Jesus. Saving belief leads to obedience, but even when we sin, we know that God "is faithful and just to forgive us our sins" when we confess (1:9).

QUOTABLE

- *Love not the world, neither the things that are in the world. If any man love the world, the love of the Father is not in him. (2:15)*
- *Behold, what manner of love the Father hath bestowed upon us, that we should be called the sons of God. (3:1)*
- *Beloved, let us love one another: for love is of God. . .God is love. (4:7–8)*
- *There is no fear in love; but perfect love casteth out fear. (4:18)*
- *Little children, keep yourselves from idols. (5:21)*

UNIQUE AND UNUSUAL

First John includes none of the usual features of a Bible letter—greetings, identification of the author, and the like. But it's a very warm, compassionate letter nonetheless.

SO WHAT?

"These things have I written. . .*that ye may know that ye have eternal life*" (5:13, emphasis added).

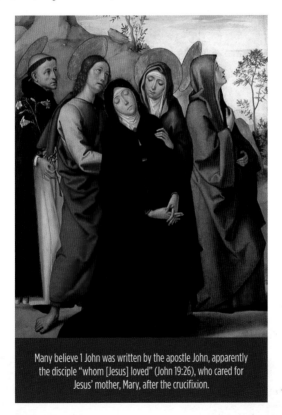

Many believe 1 John was written by the apostle John, apparently the disciple "whom [Jesus] loved" (John 19:26), who cared for Jesus' mother, Mary, after the crucifixion.

2 JOHN

Beware of false teachers who deny Jesus' physical life on earth.

AUTHOR / DATE

The apostle John according to church tradition. The author is identified only as "the elder" (1:1). Written approximately AD 92.

DETAILS, PLEASE

Addressed to "the elect lady and her children" (1:1), perhaps an actual family or, figuratively, a church, 2 John tackles the heretical idea that Jesus had not been physically present on earth. The letter may be a reaction to the "gnostics," who taught that Jesus was spirit only and that He just appeared to suffer and die on the cross. This teaching, of "a deceiver and an antichrist" (1:7), should be avoided at all costs.

QUOTABLE

• *This is love, that we walk after his commandments. (1:6)*

UNIQUE AND UNUSUAL

Second John, one of the New Testament's four single-chapter books, is the shortest by verse count: thirteen.

SO WHAT?

Just as in John's time, false teachers spread dangerous ideas in today's world. Every teaching should be weighed against scripture, 2 John says. "He that abideth in the doctrine of Christ, he hath both the Father and the Son" (1:9).

3 JOHN

Church leaders must be humble, not proud.

AUTHOR / DATE

The apostle John according to church tradition. The author is identified only as "the elder" (1:1). Written approximately AD 92.

DETAILS, PLEASE

Addressed to a believer named Gaius, 3 John praises those (like Gaius and another Christian named Demetrius) who lead in "charity before the church" (1:6). But 3 John also has harsh words for Christians like Diotrophes, "who loveth to have the preeminence" (1:9) and refuse to show kindness and hospitality to traveling evangelists.

QUOTABLE

- *I have no greater joy than to hear that my children walk in truth. (1:4)*
- *He that doeth good is of God: but he that doeth evil hath not seen God. (1:11)*

UNIQUE AND UNUSUAL

Third John, one of four single-chapter books in the New Testament, is the second shortest by verse count: fourteen.

SO WHAT?

Hospitality isn't just for the Martha Stewarts of the world—Christians are expected to feed, house, and encourage other believers, especially those who minister full-time for God. Humble service to others follows the example of Jesus Himself (see John 13:14).

JUDE

Beware of heretical teachers and their dangerous doctrines.

AUTHOR / DATE

Jude (1:1), possibly Jesus' half brother (see Matthew 13:55; Mark 6:3). Written approximately AD 82.

DETAILS, PLEASE

Jude tackles the same problem Peter did in his second letter: false teachers who were leading the early church astray. "Murmurers" and "complainers" who were "walking after their own lusts" (1:16) were apparently using the grace of God as a cover for their sinful life-styles—and encouraging Christian believers to do the same.

QUOTABLE

- *Earnestly contend for the faith which was once delivered unto the saints. (1:3)*

UNIQUE AND UNUSUAL

Jude provides details of two Old Testament events not recorded in the Old Testament: the archangel Michael's fight with Satan over the body of Moses (1:9) and Enoch's prophecy of God's judgment (1:14–15).

SO WHAT?

Satan tries to sneak "secret agents" into God's church to confuse and ultimately crush true believers. It's the job of every true Christian to "earnestly contend for the faith" as passed down by Jesus' disciples and recorded in the Bible.

REVELATION

God will judge evil and reward His saints.

AUTHOR / DATE

John (1:1), probably the apostle. Written approximately AD 95.

DETAILS, PLEASE

Jesus Christ Himself arranges for John to receive a "revelation" of "things which must shortly come to pass" (1:1). First, in chapters 2–3, Jesus gives John words of challenge and/or encouragement for seven churches—the good, the bad, and the in-between. Then the vision turns to the actual throne room of God, where a Lamb, looking "as it had been slain" (5:6), breaks seven seals from a scroll, unleashing war, famine, and other disasters on the earth. A dragon and two beasts, allied against God, arise to demand the worship of earth's people who have not been killed in the earlier catastrophes. The satanic forces and the people who follow them incur seven "vials of the wrath of God" (16:1), which bring plagues, darkness, and huge hailstones on earth. The upheaval destroys "Babylon the great," the evil and arrogant world system, just before an angel from heaven seizes Satan, "that old serpent" (20:2), and imprisons him for one thousand years. After a brief release to instigate a worldwide war, Satan is thrown into "the lake of fire and brimstone," where he will be "tormented day and night for ever and ever" (20:10). God unveils "a new heaven and a new earth" (21:1), where He will "wipe away all tears" (21:4) from His people's eyes.

The four horsemen of the Apocalypse, from Revelation 6:1–8, starting with a bow-wielding conqueror on a white horse, ending with Death on a pale horse.

QUOTABLE

- *Blessed is he that readeth, and they that hear the words of this prophecy, and keep those things which are written therein. (1:3)*
- *He that hath an ear, let him hear what the Spirit saith unto the churches. (3:22)*
- *Worthy is the Lamb that was slain to receive power, and riches, and wisdom, and strength, and honour, and glory, and blessing. (5:12)*
- *Behold, I come as a thief. Blessed is he that watcheth. (16:15)*
- *I am Alpha and Omega, the beginning and the end, the first and the last. (22:13)*
- *Even so, come, Lord Jesus. (22:20)*

UNIQUE AND UNUSUAL

Revelation is an example of "apocalyptic literature," the only such book in the New Testament. *Apocalyptic* implies "revealing secret information." The book of Revelation identifies Jesus Christ as the "Alpha and Omega" (1:8) and reveals the number 666 as a sign of "the beast" (13:18).

SO WHAT?

"I've read the back of the book," an old Southern gospel song says, "and we win!" God has given His children a preview of how this world ends—and the new-and-improved world we'll enjoy forever. The curse of sin will be gone, we'll live in perfect fellowship with the Lord Himself, and we will "reign for ever and ever" (22:5). Kind of puts our bad days in perspective, doesn't it?

Genesis: Earth, snake and apple—iStockphoto; Jacob wrestling angel—WM

Exodus: All images—iStockphoto

Leviticus: Both images—iStockphoto

Numbers: Abacus—Loadmaster (David R. Tribble)/WM; water from rock—WM

Deuteronomy: Law book and gavel—iStockphoto; Mt. Nebo Church—Tom Neys/WM; Jesus' temptation—WM

Joshua: Walls, man with camel—iStockphoto; Baal—Jastrow/WM

Judges: Statue, family—iStockphoto; soldiers—Palobserver/WM

Ruth: Photograph—iStockphoto; Ruth and Naomi illustration—WM

1 Samuel: King statue—iStockphoto; young Samuel—WM; donkey—Klearchos Kapoutsis/WM

2 Samuel: David statue—iStockphoto; Bathsheba—WM

1 Kings: Crown—iStockphoto; Solomon's worship, angel feeding Elijah—WM

2 Kings: Ruined city—iStockphoto; Elijah and chariot of fire—WM

1 Chronicles: David playing harp—WM

2 Chronicles: Solomon and queen of Sheba—WM

Ezra: Priest and scroll—iStockphoto; wedding rings—Image*After

Nehemiah: Bricklayer—iStockphoto; walls of Jerusalem illustration—WM

Esther: Woman image—iStockphoto; Esther painting—WM

Job: Man in field—iStockphoto; suffering Job, Job restored—WM

Psalms: Harpist—iStockphoto; soldiers—Yoninah/WM

Proverbs: Scroll—iStockphoto; Solomon's wisdom—WM; Solomon's wives—The Yorck Project/WM

Ecclesiastes: Lone man, seasons—iStockphoto; women in garden—WM

Song of Solomon: Both images—iStockphoto

Isaiah: Man's feet, Babylonian lion—iStockphoto; Isaiah's anointing—Jojojoe/WM

Jeremiah: Potter—iStockphoto; book burning—Patrick Correia/WM

Lamentations: Crying boy—iStockphoto; Jeremiah sculpture—Deror Avi/WM

Ezekiel: Green leaf—iStockphoto; Ezekiel's vision—WM

Daniel: Lion—iStockphoto; Shadrach, Meshach, and Abednego, Daniel in the lions' den—WM

Hosea: Bound woman—iStockphoto; Hosea—WM

Joel: Locust swarm—iStockphoto

Amos: Shepherd's staff—iStockphoto

Obadiah: Twins—iStockphoto

Jonah: Whale—iStockphoto; Jonah in Sistine Chapel—WM

Micah: Both images—iStockphoto

Nahum: London—WM

Habakkuk: Quiet woman—iStockphoto

Zephaniah: Firefighter—Andrea Booher/ Federal Emergency Management Agency/ WM; Hezekiah—David Castor/WM

Haggai: Drought—iStockphoto; Darius—WM

Zechariah: Messiah's feet—iStockphoto; Passion Play—George Grantham Bain Collection, Library of Congress

Malachi: Frayed rope—iStockphoto

Matthew: Coins—iStockphoto; John the Baptist—The Yorck Project/WM; Sermon on the Mount—WM

Mark: Jesus reaching out—iStockphoto; disciples in boat, Jesus' arrest—WM

Luke: Stethoscope—iStockphoto; Jesus at Emmaus—WM; Jesus and centurion—The Yorck Project/WM

John: Clay jars—iStockphoto; Trinity—Laurom/WM; raising of Lazarus/WM

Acts: Fire—iStockphoto; Pentecost, Saul of Tarsus—WM

Romans: Colosseum—Aaron Logan/WM; Paul—WM

1 Corinthians: Church—iStockphoto; Temple of Apollo—Ixnay/WM

2 Corinthians: Both images—iStockphoto

Galatians: Law books—iStockphoto; column—WM

Ephesians: Hands on Bible—iStockphoto; baby—Azoreg/WM

Philippians: Both images—iStockphoto

Colossians: Whispering—iStockphoto; children with letter—German Federal Archive/WM

1 Thessalonians: Christ—WM; street preacher—Adam Smith/WM

2 Thessalonians: Carpenter—iStockphoto

1 Timothy: Both images—iStockphoto

2 Timothy: Scrolls—iStockphoto

Titus: Church tower—iStockphoto; Minotaur—Marsyas/WM

Philemon: Chain—iStockphoto; reward poster—WM

Hebrews: Crucifix—iStockphoto; dead Christ, Eric Liddell—WM

James: Both images—iStockphoto

1 Peter: Burning church—Muzsi Endre-El d/ WM; Noah's family—WM

2 Peter: Con man—iStockphoto; Peter's crucifixion—The Yorck Project/WM

1 John: Both images—WM

2 John: Jesus on cross—WM

3 John: Bread in basket—iStockphoto

Jude: Tug of war—iStockphoto

Revelation: Sign—iStockphoto; four horsemen—WM

WM=Wikimedia